The Gasconade Review Presents:

Strange Gods of the Prairie

Edited by John Dorsey and Jason Ryberg

Spartan Press

OAC BOOKS
OSAGE ARTS COMMUNITY

Spartan Press
Kansas City, MO
spartanpresskc@gmail.com

OAC Books
Belle, MO
www.osageac.org

Copyright © Jason Ryberg, 2021
First Edition 1 3 5 7 9 10 8 6 4 2
ISBN: 978-1-952411-70-0
LCCN: 2021944563

Design, edits and layout: Jason Ryberg, John Dorsey

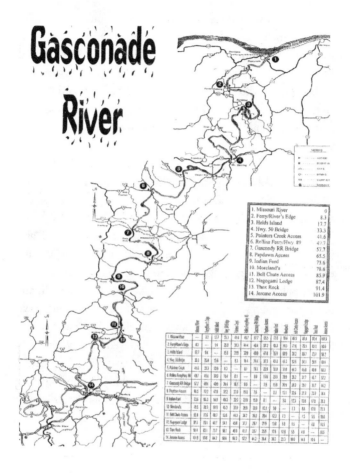

Gasconade River

1. Missouri River	0
2. Ferry/River's Edge	8.3
3. Helds Island	17.7
4. Hwy. 50 Bridge	33.3
5. Painters Creek Access	41.6
6. Rolling Ferry/Hwy. 89	49.7
7. Gascondy RR Bridge	57.7
8. Paydown Access	65.5
9. Indian Ford	73.6
10. Moreland's	78.6
11. Belt Chute Access	85.9
12. Nagogami Lodge	87.4
13. Thox Rock	91.4
14. Jerome Access	101.9

The **Gasconade River** is about 280 miles (450 km) long and is located in central and south-central Missouri in the United States. The Gasconade River begins in the Ozarks southeast of Hartville in Wright County and flows generally north-north-eastwardly through Wright, Laclede, Pulaski, Phelps, Maries, Osage and Gasconade counties, through portions of the Mark Twain National Forest. It flows into the Missouri River near the town of Gasconade in Gasconade County.

The name Gasconade is derived from "Gascon", an inhabitant of the French region of Gascony. The people of that province were noted for their boastfulness. It was applied by the early French to the Indians living on its banks who bragged about their exploits. The name means to boast or brag, and thus the river received its name. The waters of the river are boisterous and boastful and the name is also descriptive.

The headwaters of the Gasconade are in the southeastern corner of Webster County northeast of Seymour, Missouri where it drains the eastern margin of the Springfield Plateau at approximately 37°11'54"N 92°41'44"W. The river joins the Missouri River at the city of Gasconade at 38°40'28"N 91°32'55"W The river follows a meandering course through the Ordovician age dolostone and sandstone bedrock of the Ozark Salem Plateau creating spectacular bluffs and incised meanders along the way. Numerous springs and caves occur within the drainage area and along the river course. Significant tributaries include the Osage Fork of Webster and Laclede counties and Roubidoux Creek and Big Piney River of Texas and Pulaski counties. The Roubidoux and Big Piney flow respectively along the west and east boundaries of Fort Leonard Wood which lies a short distance south and east of the Gasconade.

The plateau surface near the midpoint is 300 feet (91 metres) above the river bottom near the river midpoint northeast of Waynesville creating scenic river bluffs. At the junction with the Missouri the river bottom is about 400 feet (120 m) lower in elevation than the old plateau surface above the river. The elevation of the plateau rim at the headwaters is at or above 1,600 feet (490 m) with local hilltops at over 1,700 feet (520 m) (second highest elevation in Missouri near Cedar Gap). The elevation at the confluence with the Missouri is 500 feet (150 m) giving an overall drainage basin relief of 1,200 feet (370 m).

It is ranked with a difficulty of I and II (seldom) by those who canoe, kayak and float. It is considered a good float stream because there's typically not a heavy congestion of boats. It is common to go for many miles without seeing another boat.

There are caves and an abundance of wildlife along the river and is considered a popular place by anglers for its largemouth bass and smallmouth bass.

The Gasconade River is the longest river completely within the boundary of Missouri. It has been called one of the world's crookedest rivers.

The *Gasconade Review* is a literary and arts publication based out of the Osage Arts Community (http://osageac.org/), located on the Gasconade River, just outside of Belle, Missouri. It appears twice annually, focusing primarily, but not exclusively, on writers and artists from the region and state, but occasionally also features *folks what ain't from around here.* All submissions must be hand delivered between the months of April and October and the hours of 3pm to 6pm. A decent bourbon is appreciated. Proper river attire required. Don't worry, the dogs won't bite.

TABLE OF CONTENTS

SCOTT SILSBE

HOLLY DAY

JAMES DUNCAN

LINNET PHOENIX

CHARLIE BRICE

JOHN A. CLAYTON

JASON MAYER

STEVE BRISENDINE

BRENDA LINKEMAN

PAUL KONIECKI

R. NIKOLAS MACIOCI

LINZI GARCIA

WILLIAM SHELDON

SCOTT SILSBE

Path of the Flood

We're all singin' a song that Bobby wrote—"22 is a road,
not a gun…"—and talking about strip clubs, which ones
are gone forever, which ones are still standing but empty,
closed, with future uncertain. We can't remember if it was
Cheaters or Streakers that was up on Route 30. "Streakers
is for sale, I think," one of us says. And Bobby tells us all
about the drive-thru strip club that he drove through once.
We pass a place called Nanty-Glo and I say, "Nanty-Glo"
out loud just to say it and I hear JB in the passenger seat
say it too. I suppose people like us just like to say things.
This here is a road trip during a pandemic. We won't be
able to see the insides of buildings, but we're going up
to where the old manmade lake was, to follow the path
of the flood down to where it destroyed the city, then
go up the hill to where the dead of the flood are buried.
On the drive back, we pass the Jonnet Flea, a giant old
flea market building, where people are setting tables up
out front. JB says he once got some old newspapers there
about The Flood. He says he'll show them to us sometime.

One Night at Mariani's Pleasure Bar
with Bart Solarczyk

All of my memories are going—but I think I still have a few.
We went to a reading at the old Book Exchange or The Whale,
stopping off at your car for a little smoke and some Son Volt,
then walking the couple of blocks back to Liberty and the bar.
I think I ordered an Oberon draft and I think you followed suit.
The bartend asked if we were eating and you said you'd look
at a menu. And I think eventually you ordered fried calamari
for us to share. I know that we talked about the small press—
of your memories of the '80s and '90s when Nimmo was still
up in Detroit, and Mark Weber was around, and Androla was
still reading out, and Harry Calhoun did his *Pig in a Poke* or
Pig in a Pamphlet. I think you told me again about how you
have a bin or two of correspondence and old zines and mags,
your letters from Judson Crews, your copy of the Bukowski
chapbook that Nimmo published. How you'd have to crack
those open some day to show me. Stories about the old days.
The night Zen snuck the nitrous tank into Hemingway's Bar
for the reading in the back room, how some of the wait-staff
were hitting the tank too and fucking up everybody's orders.
And maybe you told me the story of your 40th birthday party.
It's kind of blurry. But that's what I think I can remember.
Us drinking at the bar at Mariani's. Surrounded by overhead
television screens telling us what was going on in the world
beyond the glass windows of the bar. And us ignoring them.
Not wanting that information—not caring about it one bit.
Paying attention to the conversation. The stories. Our beers.

A Note from Kristin Naca Tucked in an Old Copy of *The Branch Will Not Break*

I know right where it is—in which room, on which bookcase
and on which shelf of that bookcase. And that isn't always
how it goes. Sometimes I'll scramble for hours in my place
looking for a book, a record, or some small scrap of paper.

It's a first edition, ex-library, no dust jacket. And I believe
my mother got it for me at John King in Downtown Detroit.

The bookplate on the front pastedown indicates that it was
withdrawn from Marygrove College. The "Due Date" label
on the rear flyleaf indicates the last check-out was in 1988.

I wonder now, in 2020, who decided to withdraw this book
from the library back in the late 80s or early 90s, decided it
to be a volume the library did not need on hand any longer.

Tucked in at "Lying in a Hammock…"—and of course at
that poem—is Naca's short, handwritten note, scrawled in
her neat cursive on the back of a scrapped photocopy from
a book entitled *Transcendental Wordplay*. Her note reads,

"S.S.—The one day you're not around! ♥ KNaca"

The note now must be over 15 years old—closing in on 20.
It's just a little thing. A scrap of paper. A bookmark now.

But I love how it can remind me of those days years ago. The days and nights. Those memories. Of times far gone and away. Not to say that they were the best times ever. Just different. Just not now. Vivid images I can conjure— riding on the back of Naca's motorcycle on Fifth Avenue, or at a small party in some apartment dancing with Emily. Or maybe at Brandon's place with Bruce Lee looking on as Brandon did his impression of all four guys from U2.

Time, time. Always time. The world spins its ugly spins until it finds something beautiful again. And it carries on.

It carries on.

HOLLY DAY

The Way the Story Ends

I took my shoes off before stepping on the grass so that it knew
I didn't want to hurt it, and in turn, it would fold back over my
    footprints
as though I'd never passed. When there was enough distance
between me and the house, I threw down a comb
that grew into a forest of trees, threw down a mirror
that spread into a lake too wide to swim across.
When the water filled with swans, I told them to tell the man
who would wake and come to the bank and ask
that I'd fallen into the water and drowned, he'd come too late.

When the cock finally began crowing and the sun had come up
there was enough distance between me and my old life
that not even a house built on chicken legs would be able to catch me
not even a deer with the heart of a man would be able to follow me
not even a wolf with a belly full of village children and old women
would be able to pick up my scent
not even an eagle would be able to fly high enough to find me
a tiny dot running against the spread of green prairie,
far away on the other side of the world.

I am as free as a girl raised by sparrows and butterflies.
I am as free as a girl raised by fireflies and starlight.
I am as free as my mother always wished I could be.

Genesis

Arms reach out, fill a sky that may or may not yet be
comets streak from fingers that may or may not be
holding the sun like a shield against the empty radio waves of space,
the constant black, the constant noise
this is. This is not.

There are eyes open to this, or perhaps they are shut
imagining possibilities with each breath that may or may not
be inhaled or exhaled, planets unfurl into being
spring from nightmares, this is a dream. This is real.

Skin blisters as universes and allegories
simultaneously burst into flames,
there is something coming there is nothing this
is an ending. Let's begin with this.

Of the Long Way

I'm in love with the lonely ones, the hairy jungle children that watch
from beneath the wide spread of green leaves and vinery, clutching rocks
smeared with feces and coconuts meant for throwing. Angry and violent
they are wrapped in thoughts of consequence and self-loathing.

There is a Heaven waiting for them, someplace safe from
people like me. If they come close enough, I will give them duct tape
and gauze to heal their wings, teach them to walk upright how to act
worthy of God. There are stars waiting for them, just past the clouds

once they remember they can fly.

JAMES DUNCAN

Strange Gods of The Prairie

in the south Texas night across
vast plains sloping gradient toward the sea,
towers of emaciated steel wait in the dark, calling
out with pulsating lights, mendicant prayers
offered toward passing cars and trucks
on yonder highway heading south toward
the coastal towns or northward into
the city of San Antonio, an orange dome
of light on the horizon

the towers flash in sequence, little thunderbolts
at midnight separated by barbed wire,
hard yellow dirt, tumbleweed and stone
and the forever hours between dusk and dawn,
begging the little glowing insects on that highway yonder
to peel away from their journey to join them
in the immense nothingness

beyond the stars and the moon and the
sweeping horizon, the towers stare off toward the cities
of the plain, sights they'll never see,
burning sources of power sucking their lifeforce away
through cables and wire, leaving them
erect and alone towering over fields of dead cotton
and rusted, oily pumpjacks turning idle
in the hot wind

their morse code refrain
their pleading flash of white
their unrequited dream
of more

of elsewhere

the cars and trucks pass by in the night
and children watch from windows, watch the
flickering lights, ask their parents what it all means, only
to hear hoarse whispers from the front seat:
go on now, back to sleep, there are miles
to go before home

then nothing but miles of night
small trailers with television antennae
stucco homes along a crippled arroyo
closed gas stations of black neon

then looping highway ramps
a billboard for divorce lawyers
a bbq franchise with one car in the drive-through

the subtle signs of a city rising
against the tide of night,
the orange dome now surrounding
those highway travelers and dreaming children,
some of them forgetting all they'd seen
on their long journey,
and some of them dreaming still,

of that pulsing call in the night, a language
they could not translate but understood deep
in their marrow, their synapses,
a proclamation from strange gods of the prairie
standing alone in the night and waiting their chance
for a future all their own.

A Dying Orchid on Fire

she drinks wine in her hotel room
a dying orchid on fire
watching the bottles go down

through the long alley of life
there are doors shut to us all,
hewing a singular path scarred by
lamppost lights razing the night
at the final end of the final alley
where the rain machine guns the skin
of the flat dark sea, waiting for us all

she will dive the depths,
down into the grip and the swell
letting go of shoes and sense,
waterlogged cigarettes,
pictures slipping from the heart

the darkness within the dark

the rippled along the skin of the sea
rain on the window of an empty hotel,
bed unmade,
wine dried to dust,
her ghosts only now coming to life

eager to bloom like smoke
from a candle
blown out too soon.

Two Chairs on the Front Patio

this horizon is a bandsaw churning
through the days and hours of
sunlight, moonlight, riptide clouds
pulling at the blue and the black
and the road dust billows up
to me every time a car passes by
this lonely motor inn at the edge
of the two lane highway, not
even a highway, just a flat swath
of land between some town where
everyone is trying to leave
and another town where everyone
is trying to leave, or at least hold on
until the sun sets and never rises
but even when that does finally happen
we can always walk inside this motel
and leave our two chairs on the
front patio, the little table between
them with the empty beer and
cigarette stubs, and we'll shut the
door, lie down together, let the wash
of TV flow over us, no signal,
just static now as the world stops
spinning on its axis, room service
cancelled, the lamp clicking off
and the silence of empty rooms
all around us, save for crickets,

the wind, and your heartbeat
dovetailing my heartbeat as we stare
into the darkness together
and wait.

Tonight

As the sun flips to dip-bulb-lit,
the upside down ocean
sky falls
into dusk attire.
Darkened highlights
bleed cerulean down
gold tiara burnt skyline,
fish hooked gaze
holds sway in this hush.

Look beyond the Rubicon.
This event horizon
canters westward away
from muddy estuary
mood swings,
cavorting star-spun spray.
Rippling blood orange clouds
across Atlantic peaks.
Surfing silently
the east of your west
to recline on a stone rose
with a mind-blowing kiss.

Lockdown

Nobody told the prong-tailed swallows
that international air space was closed,
that the truth dawned, the danger freedom
of movement had finally been exposed.

Nobody boycotted the wild grey geese.
Placards waved in semaphore at the sky
demanding to know why they flouted laws
made on the faces of panicked sages.

Nobody blockaded the Atlantic salmon.
Damming up the rivers' wide openings,
pulling up fish ladders to stop them,
to watch them dying, unfulfilled promises.

Nobody banned the glass eels' departure.
Locking down in the Bermuda triangle,
sealing off edges of the Sargasso sea,
preventing annual continental invasion.

Nobody told me that a moment may pass.
That I might have missed my slim chance
to fly like a migrating bird on gut instinct
chasing the setting sun as it ran past me.

Make The Connection

So this is what it becomes.
Not a supernova explosion,
shockwaves shaking the cores
of planets waiting for Armageddon.

Not the fluted song of the nightingale,
a last night at the proms style
soprano aria.

This small voice stuttered to a silence
waited for the call, for the world
to make the connection to your God.

Only the buzz of brimming nothing,
dial tone on a broken brain
that failed to convey
a muscle heart's convulsion.

Let the carrion crows pick the bones
clean, once the small feathers
have been blown clear away.

CHARLIE BRICE

Enlightenment

They say the only Zen you'll find
at the top of a mountain is
the Zen you brought with you.

They say you'll be enlightened when
you discover that your starting point
was your goal all along.

I think of the drunken guru that Ginsberg
loved like a mother; Trungpa, who
made W.S. Merwin and his girlfriend
strip naked against their will at Naropa
in 1975.

I think of Sogyal Rinpoche, at a spiritual retreat,
confronted by a young woman with whom
he had illicit sex—how the Dali Lama,
who was standing next to him,
broke down and cried.

I think of the unending spiritual quest
we all embark upon because we don't
want to admit that when it's over, it's over,
that death isn't just a dark room or an endless
sleep, but the absence of dark, the abolition of sleep.

Martin Buber averred that "all real living
is meeting," right now, with those around us.

Kurt Vonnegut wrote that, in this life,
"there is only one rule...God dam it,
you've got to be kind."

Charlie Brice says: After you wring out
your washrag of religion, hang it up
with all your other hang-ups.

Flashcuts

In the backseat of our old Oldsmobile
      two fresh pencils, unsharpened,
long, yellow,

I push one down my throat.
      I'm two years old
and don't have words like
      emergency room, esophagus, choke.

Forty years later, a tense time in an English restaurant,
      while I work a fishbone out of my throat.

I climb up a high chair, maybe three years old,
      to grab my mother's "diet pills."
I chew them with glee,
      as if they were jellybeans.

My vocabulary doesn't include *stomach pump,*
      amphetamines, unconscious.

When language fails feeling prevails—
      A lifelong fear of choking,
         my conviction of how it will end.

When there are no words,
      there's only psychic skin.

We All Know the End but Where Is the Middle?

A question asked by Jim Harrison
in his novel, *Dalva*.

It's in the backyard where the squirrels
have decimated our tulips but we smile,
shake our heads, in disgust, in delight:
we love both squirrels and tulips.

It's in Judy's conviction that there's an
hallucinogen buried in a tulip's ovary
because after eating a blossom one squirrel
dances wild across the yard, does

summersaults and backflips in midair.
I tell Judy that squirrel's been
crazy for years which makes me
wonder how long squirrels live.

The middle appears when the Forsythia
survives an April 1 blizzard—nature's
little April fools joke, and it's in
the magnolia's pink blossoms burned

umber in death by the freeze. It's
there when Judy scoots along in her
wheelchair, makes omelets even while
in pain, her eyes puddles of calm,

her voice the symphony of my life.
We are always in the middle, Jim,
until we reach the end.

To My Relatives Who Died Before COVID

To my father who loved the distance. Loved being far from things. From us.

To my other-city sister, who slumped sudden over a flip phone and wouldn't be able to mute.

To my mother, always lipstick, always powder. A mask would not have stopped her, *because,* she'd say, *people know.*

To my grandmother, flu of '18, who knitted and baked and ended up vision loss and hearing loss and that was her shelter in place.

To my free spirit aunt, who wouldn't have stayed home nohow and rather she'd slip out to one of those bars with takeout only, her in the alley with her son's best friend, the two of them not hearing my uncle's muffled footsteps.

All of them not believing. We can't see it. All of them standing on a beach, looking at the horizon that swallows everything. Look! They might say, *A whole boat hidden behind my thumb!*

When Supper Was a Thing

Not dinner, but six o'clock supper.
My mother, tending to a roast at the oven,
faint film of sweat on her forehead.
How I didn't know that she was alive
with a whole other life. How I couldn't
imagine that the strings of the apron tied
around her waist hugged her like the arms
of her secret lover.

And why would I know? I knew nothing
about men. Or even boys. Childhood was saying
eyes front. You're only 11. And yes, there
was still time for all that drama, before
I would see my father as a robbed man,

a man who would soon stoop over, heart attack
and never find out how my mother slipped off
Thursday nights, perfume in her hair, serving us
something extra quick, Hamburger Helper or
leftover roast. No way to guess how full
of tricks six o'clock supper really was.
Salt giving everything flavor, red dye giving
our food the color of hearts, our family sitting
at the table, everyone sharing the same exact meal.

When I Think About Jake

I think of him drop-kicked across the couch,
Freshman dorm. Him coming back from a mixer

where the punch was spun with vodka. He'd
sleep it off, and when he woke, we'd talk to him

for hours, me and Julie, whose baby would end up
having Jake's eyes. Julie would say that Jake's a goof

and everyone knows it, but that didn't stop love from
smacking her in the heart. I wanted to warn her, but

didn't, and six months later, Jake was needle-
dead. Julie would sleep in the scoop on the couch where

Jake had flopped himself so many times. By now, her belly
had swollen into a face. When she tossed and turned,

I could hear her dreams where Jake had his ropey arms
around her, swinging her dosey-doe, the spin of it

getting her passion-drunk. When she woke up, she would
shake her head, throw words like *shame* and *potential*

into the air, let them sail like a football and splat to the floor.
Now, she calls out of nowhere. Twentieth reunion, and do

I want to go? We haven't talked in forever, and she texts
me a photo of her son, grown now, with Jake's gangly arms,

only trackless. I think how sometimes the past can be fun,
Only not when it's a sick I finally got cured of. Not when

the echoes of what I should have told her, and told her again
if she didn't hear it the first time. Walk away from it, another

echo is saying, only this time it's for me. It's for Julie.
And even, in a way, for Jake, whose ghost still hovers

above us all, an invisible hand ready to press itself down.

MARC OLMSTED

Night & the City

Thom on the phone in San Francisco says coyote sightings on the
    downtown streets
"how's that for dystopic?"
we expect the Midwest to fall hard in the contaminated blood of Christ
happy Easter happy Beltane
and I have pulled in the trash cans
sitting now of the couch, back to the plate glass world of disease
wondering if the Left Coast will seal off intruders like the Canadian
    border
and the TV horror of bodies
in Ecuador
wrapped in blue tarp on the sidewalk
- in Italy wood coffins a Dracula factory - the priest in black face
    mask splashing with holy water
Michigan - a defiant young woman holds up a sign in a car I
    REFUSE TO COMPLY to the shelter-in-place lockdown
noir on the TV Night & the City
soon the news again after my meditation practice
Corona-a-go-go
MSNDisease.

Great White Virus

not enough sleep
listening to Moby Dick audio book
stretched out on the couch -
Ahab is President
poet as Ishmael
virus white whale America
that promised a triumph's
fake hope to the mad Captain.

Vortex of the COVID World

The strap on
my surgical mask broke
& my robber kerchief
kept slipping in the
vast tension
of the white-lit
superstore.

ACE BOGGESS

Total Honesty

I want to know about your lovers,
offer in return my history
of violence & drug abuse,
prison bars metaphor
for running in place to change locations.
How much truth can you handle?
Constant aches of ankles, knees,
sciatica? Stomach ulcers &
bloody stool? There's a pill for this,
a salve for that, none
for masks I wear where they leave scars
along the human face.
I'll share my anxieties, short-
sighted hold on grief
like a man who forgets by breakfast
that his mother passed in the night
because bacon smells better than tears.

49th Birthday

Step out of the shower, half-asleep,
Warren Zevon's "Poor Poor Pitiful Me"
shaking the sheetrock, stereo jacked,
would seem the perfect song
for starting another year, pandemic flaming,
political strife insidious pressure on my chest,
not to mention quirks of all my normal me.

No, I've had a good twelve months:
successes in career & body, awards, new books,
friends who find pleasure when misery applies
as I've been doing throughout 2020,
exploring a better life the closer death approaches
with its poisons & spycraft, &
this morning, before I finished my coffee,

I watched the Nobel Prize committee
announce the Literature laureate.
Though I couldn't understand most words,
I recognized *American & Louise Glück,* &
though I wished it were me,
I thought it a good start for my new year
to see bigwigs get this one thing right.

Magic Hour

This morning, I couldn't find the newspaper
that hid under a wet pile of brownish-yellow leaves,
a Summer snake wrapped in plastic
escaping chill & damp of Fall.

This morning was that perfect mix of light & shade
that shakes the outdoors out of focus:
all colors one color, all shapes one shape,
lenses of eyes unable to matrix
even the most indecent forms out of clusters.

This morning, I walked back & forth along the path,
feet snapping a hundred spines,
acorns like ankles popping,
noise in the vacancy, & the newspaper's recent redesign
has left it smaller, harder to locate,
less newsworthy, readily overlooked.

This morning, I plumbed the passage of night for clues
until there it was: thin rectangle
appearing from absence:
simple to disappear an object;
bringing it back is where the miracle happens.

TANYA RAKH

The Open Road

everyone wants the open road
that lonely, freezing highway
everyone wants the blood drums
the thunder flooding back

everyone wants the mortar here
to crush the wings of insects
everyone wants the end
tarred fairy-tale apocalypses
reverberating blood drums
it's dark in here
the drums are clean

all drums clean rhythm to a saw bone
a strange insect outside, those wings turn powder under fragile snow
each flake stands on end like hair like spine like tidal wave this time
glistening rabbits, hungry boys, wide-eyed girls asunder in torn
dresses, all the lights and spines and rabbits swallow thunder on the
bone road, in the bone dream. the drums still clean

it rained the other day, here under the thunder, freezing bone road
to highway, slick-jawed destiny. up some tar mountains and past
the infinity horizon she shakes teeth with sad devils on an overpass.
they sit and drink awhile, always a bottle or two of that thickness.
soon say their goodbyes, trace lit constellations back to city

back to city, back to skeleton
it's dark in here
the tails of star apocalypses

everyone wants the open road
those crackling, peeled-back highways
everyone wants the salt.

Tamiami

palm clusters in an alleyway
of a backwater star
no apologies in this climate
abandoned dogs chase down
barefoot cold mosaic

sure you don't want a ride, little lady?
he loops again this grimy highway

follows me down rot citrus turns
all blinds drawn, shotgun tooth and
spinning dehydration
better walk faster, girl,
these lights can kill

(within thin windows
I shiver cruel February
red currents
knot my shoulders)

sunburnt land creatures
scuttle backwards over paradise
what's tomorrow, paradise?
we rot in crocodile mouths

I'll be the ocean this time
waves against my ribcage
hydrogen to my satellite.

He Wrote Such Good Poems

you move and pose just like a model
and you are not afraid to scream

I've always been afraid to scream
to use my voice too loudly
I whisper from the corners
mummified
in mirrored spiderwebs

you are not afraid to break in public
to twitch and wail and almost die
someone always scrapes you
from beneath the trees
I always follow you beneath the trees
I help you not to die

why do I help you not to die?

you are not afraid to hate
to melt me into plaster, bruise
my ligaments and verse
you eat me dead and whole
but always sing such lovely solos . . .

plastic rubble creatures
my guitar a bleeding spine
air once heavy is heavy still but
hollowed
you and I against the noise
of silent furniture.

LINDA ROCHELEAU

Pandemonium

Clothes tumble in a dryer.
Lint gathers, as usual. The morning
paper arrives with a harsh thud
on the porch sagging with weight of the house.
T.V. a harbinger, a lament, of calculations.
Number of new cases, recoveries, death.
Mainly, death. Death. Death. Death.
Death. Death. Death. Death. Death
Death. Death. Death. Death. Death.
A drumbeat, a rattle, a rhythm.
Later, at Wal-Mart, a prepper, in a
CBRN mask, its yellow shield, a glare
unloads his cart. The bulge in his
camouflage reveals he is carrying.
First, gallons of milk, eggs. Crates of
rodent and roach killer, interceptor
boots. His day finally reaches fruition.
You can't make this stuff up. I edge
my cart up slightly, mainly snacks,
various emollients and beauty products,
chicken breasts, pizza, Ben and Jerry's,
cat litter. He cast back a furtive look.
A survivalist caught in a panorama.
Shoppers clinging to their carts.
Shelves laid bare like gaping jaws.

Conceal and Carry

We carry
sustenance in baskets
fresh from Trader Joe's.
Burdens of our friends
or elders, weight of
our children. It's what
we conceal that
defines us.

On Meeting a Dead Poet at Dawn

Startled awake
by a technicolor dream
ending with a message
to Gerry Locklin scribbled
on a strip of paper, narrow
as a sparrow's life. All
starts and high wire escapes.
The message profound
but lost to first shadow
of morning. Locklin
a towering presence,
receptive and sheltering.
Lots of cats. Neon pink
and aquamarine. Flotillas
of artists waving banners.
Beaders, glassblowers,
poets and lancers,
dressed in scarves
and pantaloons.
The air a sheen
of silk and sherry.
Merriment abounded.
I stayed awhile
uninvited
yet honored.

MELA BLUST

Wild Things

i once drove by
an eight-point buck
walking right down
the middle of the road

the sodium lights
bathing his antlers
in a musky orange glow

as i passed
i slowed down
to look at him and
he, too, slowed
to look at me

i think we both knew
the other
was just as wild.

Romance

on our first date, he was
a perfect gentleman
fed me strawberries
and held my hand

on our second date
the tension between us
balanced like the beads of
sweat on our brows

he said he wanted me
in the worst way-
so i got sloppy blackout drunk
tangled myself up in his sheets
and fell asleep

i don't know
if that's what he meant
but he's never complained

and we both know
my worst
is also my best.

Faith

i lay my head down
on your chest
listening to the powerful thudding
of your heart

and although you passed
your last physical
with flying colors

to suddenly think
that the fist-sized organ
i'm hearing
is responsible for the livelihood
of every inch
of the person i love most

is too fragile
to believe.

LUIS CUAUHTEMOC BERRIOZABAL

Begging Memory

She wears out the spoons
she uses as mirrors; she
lights up every room as
she walks with candles in
hand; she has the softest
touch unlike that of a corpse;
look in her eyes on any
given day and witness calm
and storms; the old soul in
her young face is soothing;
the first time I saw her I
begged my memory never
to leave me; in a jar of bees
she kept she was the honey.

In My Awkward Way

I came to you as a stranger.
My intentions were good.
I was out of the wilderness
that filled my life for years.

I came with a hunger for
friendship in my awkward way.
I had a notion we'd click
and I was compelled to try.

With my soul out of its hell
and thirsting for kindness,
I sought out a beautiful
soul from a position of need.

My eyes filled with wonder
in the times I spent with you.
It happened so slowly.
A great friendship was born.

I now have somebody who
has a beautiful soul. I feel
the sweetest taste on my tongue
and sunlight so bright and
my speech is all glossolalia.

The Bright Children of the Sky

I watch them in the water's reflection,
the bright children of the sky,
whose light is perpetual at night,
it persists in our slumbers,
and when we dream it is still there.
Night would not be the same without
the stars, the moon, and the occasional
comet, and alas unexplained phenomena,
that appear to us when we are alone.

If I see an unidentified flying object,
or a Martian parachuting in the sky,
would it be fabulous or something to fear?
Would be an illusion of the eye
like the visual hallucinations of men and
women? The stars are enough for me.
I like the moon well enough.
I imagine it motionless,
the biggest child in the sky.
I watch its reflection in the water,
the sprinkled stars all around.
I watch out for the extra-terrestrials.
It is not out of the ordinary
for the horizon to reveal such things
with artificial light or intelligence
unseen to those with eyes and minds closed.

JULIE VALIN

Sunshine Coming Through

I clutch his hand
and keep to the sidewalk.

Up at the corner
a group of young guys
in street-corner cool
play their boombox.

We walk in silence,
they part like clouds,
let us
beam through.

"There goes the lucky man!"
one of them shouts
at our backs.
We glance down.

"He's got his OWN
piece of sunshine!"
another chimes in.

We cross the street,
don't look back,
their street-gray mist
folds into one,
as clouds
often do.

Playin' the Storm Out

The sky is dark and hovering low
and the cold steel wind
makes the bare branches wave
bye bye, baby, bye bye.

Everything's gone -
nothing to face what's brewing
except me and the sleeping dog,
and this old beer snuck
from the back of the fridge.

My own blues,
my own flat notes and rises
a song in the windchimes.
The sad and hopeful harmonica
of my memory
never taken out and played,
now dusted off as the clouds beat
rain drops down,
my lips humming in its teeth,
singing

ain't nobody left me
but myself....
Ain't *nobody left me*
but myself.

Another Poem Lives

He picked me up
at the Louis Armstrong Airport
followed by a failed attempt
at the Drive-Thru Daiquiri Shop
with the joint surrounded
by 6 cop cars, and the worker
being walked out in handcuffs.
Sans daiquiris, he drove me around
the Lower Garden District, pointing out shotgun
houses and Antebellum witches' mansions,
the colors and shapes, a gallery of streets,
and then an evening walk down Magazine
to the neighborhood Vietnamese place
under a vampire sky.
Now, here we are,
in his New Orleans living room,
drinking vodka & sodas out of famous glasses
etched in New Orleans architecture.
3 years gone and Little Walter
playing against the rock 'n roll hum
of the window cooler and overhead fan.
He tells me stories of his after-hours
adventures in his new adapted dialect,
with all traces of California gone.
He remains a poem
wrapped up in life.
Even his street is named after
the Greek muse of lyrical poetry,
for god's sake.

He refills our drinks
and somehow
she comes up—
he loved her,
he admits.
He still loves her.

"At least you got some damn good material," I offer.
"Yeah," he exhales in sort of a laugh,
"that material can sure keep me warm
in the middle of the night...

if I set it
on fire."

The famous glass he's holding,
sweats like tears running down
on what will now become
this famous August night,
the humid air
choking and glistening
with truth,
as the Blues
ring out
and another poem
lives and breathes.

WILLIAM TAYLOR JR.

The Night She Got Her Glitter All Over Me

The night she got her glitter all over me
she wore a flowered dress and cowboy boots

the jukebox at the Irish bar
had the gift of pardon

and we sang:

axes for the frozen seas!
axes for the frozen seas!

and the joy on her face as we danced
is a poem I lack the music to write

the night she got her glitter all over me
the sad mean world was no match

for poetry or song or the laughter
of the righteously drunken

the night she got her glitter all over me
the void was obsolete and ashamed
of its powerlessness

I'd pay a lot right now even for a
bootleg copy of the feeling of it

to play in these horrible hours
in these lonely rooms

where everything sways
and nothing sings.

Song

We wait in the dark outside
the glow of trainwrecks
and the burning cities
we always knew
these things would find us
it's just the broken sky
it's just the fire singing
the only songs it knows
it's just dust and bone
and the ghosts of the lonely
and forgotten swimming
through our blood
trying to make their way
back home
there's nothing needs saving
that will be saved
it's nothing worth mentioning
it's just the way it was written
in sand and stone
and the last look on her face
things will be quiet again
like before we were born
that beautiful silence
darling you can cry
for as long as you wish
the weeping is just a moment
a moment is just forever

cling to me in the pretty rain
until the ancient sorrow
of everything finally
finds and reclaims us
as its own.

Me & the Ghosts

There was nowhere I had to be.
It was late afternoon, I was on Market Street
in the midst of the financial district.
I was walking to the Ferry Building
for no reason other than it was a place to go.
It had bathrooms and people to look at.
It had little stores in which to buy food
and drink. People were getting off work,
rushing for buses, going in pairs and groups
to restaurants and bars. All of the girls
looked pretty, even the ones who weren't.
All the old men seemed kindly enough.
On the concrete plaza the skateboard kids
were doing their thing, sliding down railings
and weaving through throngs of people
with the grace of birds.
The people of the street stood in groups
exchanging drugs and money with a studied nonchalance.
I entered the Ferry Building, used the restroom
and bought a cup of coffee at a kiosk.
I went out to where the ferries were
and saw the people lined up to board.
I looked at the people drinking wine
and eating seafood on the restaurant patios,
talking about things they seemed pretty
sure about, businessmen slapping
each others' backs and laughing like horses.

I looked at the ocean and a few ships
that were headed somewhere.
I looked at the bay bridge, filled with cars
and trucks and buses going in one direction
or the other. I eventually got bored
and started back along Market Street
with no destination in mind.
Everything around me, the people
and the buildings, the sky and the earth
all seemed possessed of some sense
of purpose and permanence
I'd not yet seemed to manifest.
I didn't mind so much, I was used to it.
Me and the ghosts, we just drift.

GEORGE WALLACE

MEMORY OF THE CONTOURS OF A ROSE

It is almost easter, my child has not yet come, my term of
punishment is not yet complete;

I am not in my own employ, I am at the mercy of any man in
town; it is my fate to suffer any one of them, great or small,
with sufficient coin to pay for my bread;

I am a streetwalker on the outskirts of the city, a nurse,
a counselor; I sell my body to strangers, my hands, my time;
I stand at the edge of this or that one's soul and draw nightmares
from the well; and in the morning I go down to the river and wash
the grief from my bedlinens;

nursemaid to the stricken and the damned, consoler to the worst
of men!

I do these things for a living, that I may know god's purer love, as I
would know death; that I may see the face of my own unborn child
one day, and rejoice;

the serpent in my belly remembers the contours of a rose; the
leviathan that glides thru my womb recalls narrow passageways
and great open seas;

I know my place, I veil my face in shadows and in dust; place of
my birth, place of great consternation, place where there are no
olive groves or flowing waters; place where shepherds and their
flocks refuse to go, or honest men;

and they will bury me here;

and when i give birth to my own child I will do so here, on my
own terms -- in the manner of my forebears, and no other.

WHAT KABIRA SAYS

I am a raindrop in stone -
faced mountains I am
an ocean inside & contain
all possibilities I will give birth
where & whenever I please
& to what? Who knows,
not the wild goat tho
he knows how I taste
in spring, not the minnow
who orphans me as I
trickle downstream
no! not the snowy egrets
who line my shores or
the snail dart or
the fat black bear
sleeping beside me
in Alpine meadows,
dreaming salmon -
& certainly not fishermen
with their hooks & trickery,
or the people of the valleys
& plains who build too
high & too fast on my
banks (I am water I am
all about the flow, I abhor
permanence, I ruin cities as I go)
yeah I am a raindrop, I do not
stand still, I am known by
many names, like Change,
or Motion, or Anarchy -

I give birth to hurricanes
& dew, to the easy things
that do not struggle
out of the cradle (I drop
like sweet fruit from
heaven) & to hard
things too, things
which fight every step
of the way - against
gods and devils,
against gravity,
against the
roots & snags
of men (I will
give birth to floods
if I have to) & precipi-
tous canyon walls - but
otherwise I can be
calm, very calm -
calm as cattle,
I can feed the soil
that feeds Nations
if you let me & what is
more pleasant under great
open skies & along plains
tended by sober men than
to lie beside me in spring
w/ your beloved & dream --
as I go along easily to meet
my great mother, the sea.

WHITE CLOVER, HEATHER, THYME & FIR

so my lover it is spring, how easy it is to wake you like I used to
& call you by the name you revealed to me

in that other spring when we were young & lay naked in the
tender grass, alone on a hillside in Thessaly (aside from an
unsmiling

goat-herd boy) -- half a morning's walk from the village well &
gossiping women; we were clean of body, original of mind --

& spring covered us shoulder to toe in white clover, heather,
thyme & fir, so the bees would not plunder our perfect bodies
for honey;

& your young eyes blazed & my strong heart never faltered;

& we made love in
immaculate
spring

by a Thracian oak and swift running waters, while the goat-
herd played his sacred song on a pennywhistle.

TIM HEERDINK

Temporarily Fresh

It's half past two & I'm sitting here, listening
to the last hacking of blades upon blades
before winter comes with its frost.

I think of fruits forgotten now rotten
dangling on weakened stems,
waiting for the final fall.

These could've been pies or cobbler
like Mom used to make
before the earth claimed her.

Pears, apples, pecans, & blackberries
decorate the trees & brush
unlike others I refuse to cut.

Countless times staring at the blank page
have I jumped like the end has finally come
to find pecans descending on my tin roof.

I'd like to think it could be Mom
trying without fail to awaken me,
saying, *Hey, it's time to collect!*

Our world provides for us;
we should be thankful
before it's our time to return.

Deconstructing Portraits of Poets Past

after Kaveh Akbar

Achy appendages beg for ice packs
after roughly brushing black acrylic
across canvases that act
as stereotypes to describe
artists who are hard to understand.

Akbar knows the dance
a man does when he's encumbered
and stumbling with drink.
Ask me how I want my coffee
as I ponder a list of favorite
ales. He's the poet who got me
answering, *espresso with creamer.*

Alcohol is for the depressed
author who believes
authentic creativity requires
axing the weeping
angels fluttering in the pit.

Alternatives to crash reports:
assimilate, set limits,
avert your tongue
away from the suds
any time you must drive.

Paper Man

I'm just a paper man
someone cut out
& left to blow
with the wind.

You're of ivory,
the finest white
that shines like
little fairies
on a summer eve.

My crumpled parts
torn on the edges
need mending
& a break.

Your hollow
space can give
the shelter
I need.

Get me
out of this
rain.

JOHN DORSEY

Poem for Kevin Ridgeway

there is no sun or sand
to run our toes through here

just rain
that clings to the leaves
like heartbreak

a broken down walmart box
covered in tree limbs & brown grass
that refuses to move
with the morning wind

my legs feel heavy
coming up
from the mailbox

there is always someone
who's walked this path before

if nick drake listened
for the sound of birds
he'd have found them here

a woodpecker singing a sad song
on a telephone pole

letting out all of its wisdom
like a jackhammer
carving the names
of high school sweethearts
into the bark
of better lives.

Frank Stanford Makes Me Feel Lazy

the truth is
i've never kissed a girl
along the arkansas river

the dead probably consider
every winter storm
to be spanish fly

this poem should be longer
it knows nothing about generational poverty
it has never been the kind of dog
to chase its own tail
or snap its jaws at fleas
devouring the air
under a sweetgum tree
every spring

it should be made
of stronger bones.

The Glory Days of Bullying

on a school trip to kennywood
aaron kimmel spits in my hair
at least a dozen times

& laughs about it
in his ripped jimmy z t-shirt
that smells like copenhagen
chewing tobacco & sweat

& brags about how his father
gave him 60 bucks
for pizza & funnel cakes

while some weeks my dad
can't even afford
to put gas in his car
to get
to work.

Marty's Scissors

Marty took a pair of scissors and
stabbed himself in the right temple
and after they stitched him back up
and made sure all the parts
in his head still worked
he consented to voluntary treatment

it was the first time I ever met him

I asked him, "why'd you do it man?"
he said, "it's all right now"
and then asked for mouthwash

the next day when I was making rounds
I counted 14 empty bottles
next to Marty's bed
I had to explain to him that
the mouthwash
didn't have alcohol in it
Marty laughed and kept laughing
he was discharged the following day
apparently this was just something he did

the next time I saw Marty
we joked about the scissors
and his head looked much better.

Closure

the flags are
raised
full-staff
and the crow's nest
is on
fire
the altar servers
are drunk on
holy blood
and the street preachers are
involuntarily committed

i watched him
jump
from the
fourth floor window
and hit concrete
covered in rock salt
and geese shit
while i ate tuna salad
and scratched
my belly.

Intoxicated Man in an Outdated Bar Bathroom

wooden walls
leaned
against for
support
begin to
pulse,
as a
barrel bolt
on the
door
keeps the
swelling tide
away...

outside
clouds roll by
under a
purple-grey
night.

RUSTY BARNES

Whom the Gods Favor

for Sherm Barnes 1935-2016

At your graveside service I stood stunned
with drugs and the clergy member who'd

been assigned to you was like hearing
metal at a folk concert blissed-out Green-

sleeves backed with War Pigs, worse
than inappropriate. My family and I around

the dug grave waiting for something unique
to happen. Finally, I squatted and took

a handful of dirt and dropped it in the hole.
My uncle followed. And so, my father, we left

you there as my fifteen year old son finished
the burial, scraping dirt into the chasm with

a snow shovel taken from our van trunk,
my wife on her hands and knees beside him.

I suppose it's appropriate that your only
grandson buried you. I suppose like me

the others had their own ways of coping.
Yet the open wound remains. By intinction

or by cross or by the rolling away of the stone
I stay your frail fat son remembering you by

all means necessary, following in my own
inimitable way the paths all sons follow when

they face their father-gods, Christ or Heracles
or Perseus or Sherm the path of most resistance

and the redemption of the light in the face
of the dark: there is no way to outdo death.

Though I may blow my head off trying.

Day Journal 8/15/18

Rider and I walked down
    for coffee
    two larges, extra extra, one with caramel swirl.
Some munchkins for the girls.
We talked Shakespeare on the way back, feet

trudging the hard asphalt. They
recognize us now, every shift,

smile---> and have our order ready.

I love so much
being known in the community. I'm reading
Creeley's letters from India in the 40s,

how sure and confident
he was about his place in the world.
I'm twice his age then and three times
less confident.

Heather will go out tonight with Jenn
who she hasn't seen in more than 25 years
though they remain close online.

Erin. . .messaged Heather today,. First
we'd heard in days.

I fear the worst.
Looking forward to Creeley's letters
to Blackburn,
coming up in the late 40s early 50s.
I wish I had a correspondent
like that, always ready with an opinion
or   something new
to discuss.

Tonight we'll order pizza
because it's been ages
and it's blazing hot and humid,
and cooking. I don't wanna.

Dumb In America, 1986

We were listening to Berlin
at the Chemung County Fair

in a tent strip club, rainwater
running down the canvas

walls and gathering in huge
puddles near the overlarge

sound system. We sat at crude
wooden tables with purloined

beers in front of us (we were only sixteen)
watching a woman named Shara

shimmy and pirouette around
an unsolid pole. She took our breath

away, the first woman we had ever
seen with pierced genitals she was

proud of, slapping her cunt with her
chapped hand saying *you want some*

of this, boys, don't you? I know you do.
Some well-meaning shitkicker then

threw a beer on her breasts but she
remained onstage picking up the beer

and rain-sodden dollar bills. It became
a tale I told for years for which I did

not realize the full story and as I sit
here now with my wife beside me

I tell her how it was to be male and sixteen
and dumb in America, unaware of any-

thing but the end of my own prick
and somehow proud of my ignorance,

so much a redneck I might have tried
to protect her in *my* wounded pride

instead of just leaving the place so as
not to wound *her* pride any further.

In the moment I haw-hawed, content to think
I was among friends building great memories.

BRETT LARS UNDERWOOD

Down Lo

Thinking he had something to prove,
he took on the night.
He took on the noise.
He took on the hill, the beer,
the whiskey, the challenges
of the youths. He shot.
He sipped. He chugged. He left.

He fought the hill.
The hill in collusion with gravity
met the swerve. The legs
of dipsomania failed.
But, it was only when he thought
of that delicious spot behind her ear
and the memory of her laugh.
Then he lost touch. Lost concentration.
It only took a second.
No longer atop the wheels,
he kissed the concrete.
Then he ran home with the handlebar
jabbing at his ribs.

Hemingway had three wives from St. Louis.
Gertrude Stein called him on it.

O.K. Best to keep the shotgun away
from the whiskey.
Sleep late or wake early
with the working idiots.
Cover the balls
before they suffer
another wack.

Spew

More energetic and delirious than I'd been in awhile, a customer at
the bar upped the giddy with silly shit spurting forth with innocent
excitement about the world of the new.

"I'm not kidding, Violet," he said to the bartendress.

"I don't care what it is, but I like to try anything I haven't had before."

"That was good!" he said of a Huber lager. "What else you got!"

She poured him a Schlafly American Pale Ale and he piped up again.
Heads turned.

We were sipping coffee on a day that hadn't quite yet kick-started itself.
I barely got some lunch in me and was starting to long for the smoke
I had left in my flat.

The coffee bent nothingness into something but nothing and I felt
conscious for the first time since the whiskey and chronic buzz
I had put on a couple nights ago, before cold and dark days of
reading and sleeping.

"I discovered Pizza Hut all-you-can-eat," the wackadoo continued,
loud enough for all in the dining room to hear.

"Man, I had salad and nine pieces of pizza. And then! I had some
cottage cheese and some pudding!"

The cat next to me was now crying into his sleeve, trying his best
not to laugh out loud.

"Then! My buddy called and wanted me to hang some drywall
with him! Aaaahhh no, I'm immobilized!"

The shit satellite radio poured more 80s schlock into the mix. I knew I couldn't last long thinking about all the hopeless love I had spent while listening to this dreck but somehow it felt good, sparked by the coffee and an increasing need for inhalation.

"You show me an all-you-can-eat graze bar and I'm there!" he cackled now. "I wish they had a place that had it all. I'd munch cheeseburgers, souvlaki and kani maki!"

This little dude must have a tapeworm, I thought…and how does he know about sushi? He didn't look the type: a buzz cut, weathered face and work-a-day demeanor. But there was something crazy and angelic about him. He took his days with him, I guess. I don't know. I remember thinking that NOW was enough for him and he was definitely enough for all of us. He had us by the ovaries and gonads.

He let us dive down and sink into our own comments about Morrissey and the shit Brit DJ. Let us look out the windows onto the banking public on Grand Boulevard. Let us sip and wonder "what next?"

And then, "I started drinking when I was five".

Skulls on necks spun, they did.

"I used to sit on my Granddaddy's lap and drink beer, Violet."
He had us on the hook again and was reeling us back in, but I was glad that I was not him, yet jealous and envious, somehow.
"He used to give me whiskey, too! Ha Ha Ha Ha Ha Ha Ha Ha Ha Ha!"

Violet kept herself together somehow. The rest of us were either stunned or crumbling to pieces, but she was clocked in and simply grinning a little.

"Do you like that APA? That's what I drink," she said.

I liked her composure, but I wanted more.

"Ah, Man! This is fucking great! What is this????!!"

Violet pointed at the APA tap handle.

"It's kind of fruity!!" he squeaked as the boy to my left lost it, spewing mucus across his plate of partially eaten chicken wings. We all shuffled awkwardly in our spaces. I took another sip of java and looked back out the glass onto South Grand. Violet made like she had something urgent to do in the kitchen.

Belch Aplenty

Hope no one ever finds the journals
scribbled in darkest hours, long ago?
A glimmer of light, too, when wandering
and wondering about how to make it
in the world after the small-town
existentialism-gone to-university-theology,
sports failure and injury
and the re-education on the streets
and in the alleys of St. Louis
that have always been
about "who you know".
What?

Thankfully there are weirdos
and music; art and other forms
of expression, plus a bunch
of "foreign" in...flu...ences
to explore.
Not too deep,
but just say that beings
of a younger age will either face
the bullshit of this community
and figure it out or will stay
in isolation and belch bullshit.

Belch plenty of it.
Revel in it.

BUT...(and maybe this is wrong)
figure out a way to connect
without these isolated tweets
and complaints and grumpy vibes.

VICTORIA GARTON

Black Vultures

Black vultures have purchased the sky,
wing-tips stretching as far as bodies are wide,
steely beaks like extended screw-drivers.
no-neck musclemen of the air--heads off shoulders.

No chirps from small birds, a part of some other kingdom.
Heifers have gathered newborns in a copse of trees--
circled their wagons—and stand looking outward.

I wade through ragweed to hone in on the spot
where a black vulture bore through hot afternoon air.
Breathing deep for rancid afterbirth, I steel myself
for a screw hole where an eye once was.

My mind grows hard around profit and loss, but
I smell only the singed August grass, the piles of manure
turning to leather. A small yellow butterfly pollinates chicory.
What is this life defined by possession and threat?
The butterfly and I are two among many and the black vultures
have taken their drills and jack-hammers to the highway
where they harvest the roadkill and dodge the trucks.

Pileated Wood Pecker

The leash tightens. The dog
in awkward adolescence tenses
as a crest of red dips and dips
into the trunk of the wild cherry.
I whisper, "Easy."

It will be easy for the wild cherry
to crash in the next big wind and all this life—
the woman focused on the camera in hand,
the dog so transfixed he loses the dance,
the zap of white on drumming head,
the incendiary crest excavating dead wood.
the charcoal body with fury driving home
the will to shut down what, amid advancing decay,
proves to be a teeming ant factory.

The pileated woodpecker drills
the heart of death.
Ants rush off as if oblivion
were but a morning place.
The dog and I proceed.

Light Through a Cat's Ear

On the other side of the sliding door,
a grey tabby cat has positioned himself
so the sun comes pink through his ear.
If he were tame, he might carry
those triangles of rose quartz
with a haughty air
or move with regal demeanor
adorned with ears like petals from
Rosa Queen Elizabeth.

Were he a pampered cat,
he might care
that in the left ear is a small dark spot
the size of a wood tick.
It no doubt is a wood tick
and will at some future time drop
its leather-encased garnet to the grass.

TONY GLOEGGLER

Song of Solomon

Today. When your hands first
lift out of pockets, pop
open coat buttons, swing
arms lightly by your side,
you forget it's Wednesday
in February. You put a dollar
in the homeless guy's hand, grab
today's paper off the stand, walk
down subway stairs. Today,
the F train sits in the station,
waits patiently for you. You lean
against closed doors, unfold
the paper to spring training.
Gleyber Torres, this year's prize
prospect, kneels on deck,
swings a weighted bat, stares
past the center field fence.
CC twirls, throws in the bull
pen, hopes to squeeze one more
season out of his left arm. Today
you believe they'll both make it.

You lift your head, leave
Florida and discover a young
woman sitting across the car.
Long fingers push loose curls

of dark hair from her eyes, turn
and dance through pages of *Song
of Solomon.* The words brush
her lips, brighten brown eyes
with tinges of green. You want
to take her hand, get off the next
stop, rent a red corvette and gas it
up. She'll glide across the seat,
fit under your arm. The radio
will sing *Sweet Soul Music,*
you'll roll windows down as wheels
kick up speed. Today, she lifts
her eyes, finds yours and touches
you with the softest smile. You watch
her stand, step off at West Fourth.
And today, she turns, looks back,
holds you all the way to Brooklyn.

Alive on Arrival

Thirty, thirty-five years after
being called the next Dylan,
his debut album playing
on every FM radio station
and "Romeo's Tune" bulleting
up the Billboard charts, Steve
Forbert is pacing the dark stage
of a small club. He's plugging
in his own guitar, adjusting
the mic's height, strumming
a few chords and blowing
into the harmonica wired
around his neck. Almost
show time, I order an over
priced flat bread pizza instead
of the tiny Angus sliders.

Forbert opens with 'Thinkin',
a slinky shuffle tune telling us
not to spend too much time thinkin'
and thinkin' or *you'll wind up*
stranded behind. Tapping the table
to his easy rhythms and natural
melodies, I go down to Laurel
with him and his songs, spend

a week in January drinking
and driving with old home town
friends and end up sleeping
in his boyhood bed, listening
to church bells ring, wondering
what kind of guy am I really am.

Right now, I'm a guy who thinks
I'm sick of winter. I can't seem
to shake this week long cold
and I'm not in love with anyone
at the moment. I'm sitting
across from Rob and he's sipping
whiskey trying to forget he lost
his keys today, that it cost
two hundred dollars to change
the locks. My ex girl friend
in Vermont has been angry
since she found out I put
her name in my last book
of poems. We're not speaking
and I miss her son badly.

Between songs, the audience
can't help yelling out requests.
I resist the temptation to get
on my knees, beg for "I Blinked
Once," "Born Too Late." Tomorrow,

Rob will be riding the C train
to Fort Greene hoping to give
things with this young girl of his
another chance. I'm thinking
I'll send Helen another letter,
admit I messed up, apologize
again and hope she'll forgive me.

Forbert fills ninety minutes
plus two encores with a number
of instantly recognizable cuts
we all mouth the words to.
He covers Ray Davies, Jimmie
Rogers and Elton John, sprinkles
in a few album obscurities,
a bunch of new tunes he's clearly
dying to play. Maybe they won't
find their way to your car radio
or download into the ears
of all those hipsters crowded
onto the late night L train back
to Williamsburg, but Forbert
seems happy enough playing
guitar and singing his songs
while we clap, yell for more.

He stands at the bar, signs
old vinyl covers, talks, laughs
and poses for photographs

as he sells old and new CDs
until he finally says good night,
packs up his truck and heads
down the line to another joint.
And no, I'm not dreaming about
happy ever after, true true love
or even one quiet, snow falling
fireplace evening in Helen's arms
as I climb down subway stairs.
I'm thinking about the last time
I flew into Portland, wandered
around the airport and heard
Jesse call my name. I'm thinking
I'd be happy enough to fall asleep
beneath a deep pile of blankets,
an electric heater at my feet
and wake up way too early
to that silly nonsense song
Jesse hums as he lies in bed.

Undercover

Italian ladies draped in lace
placed coins in collection plates,
lit green novena candles.
German Shepherds sniffed
the wooden crutches, nuzzled
against my leg braces. Mothers
grabbed their children's hands,
whispered, "Don't stare."
When they walked away,
I flipped them the finger,
shut my eyes and turned
my braces into airplane wings,
my crutches into machine guns.
I swooped down, fired
round after round and flew
home with my thumbs raised.
I sat on our fire escape
making no sounds and trying
to blend into the background
like a spy. I imagined it was me
picking teams for stickball,
hitting Spaldeens two sewers long
and racing around the bases
like a skinny black kid.
Nighttime, I slipped under
the covers with a flashlight,
wrote in tiny notebooks. Careful

not to let my pencil scratch
against the paper. Afraid
someone could see that spec
of light, read my words. Afraid
they had ways to make me talk.

JASON BALDINGER

For Patrick Beard and The Rusty Razors

this poem is for patrick beard
and the rusty razors
who played barefoot
on one leg
to an empty bar
on a red river tuesday
an off night for musical tourism

my last name got recognized
it had nothing to do with a candy store
as I walk down 6th
sunday afternoons cheers
echo as my cousin centers
the line while danny white
gets ghosted by history
irma thomas covers
rattle the windows
duck in for a beer

the next venue
the next beer
the next venue
the next beer
repeat til neon swims
repeat until patrick beard
the rusty razors

finish their first set
to an empty bar

I've played to empty rooms
read to scatters of people
in more places I can count
it's a sobering experience

I can't leave empty bars
while a band plays
if there is no one to witness
did these moments exist

before the second set
beard buys me a beer
he knows I can't runaway

but this band is insufferable
barely competent jug band
or off night it's your dime

west texas hellscapes await
grinding metal and sunshine
my stomach and head
will not be the youth of tomorrow

there's enough gas stations
to make it across the endless
without having to bury a roadside shit
like a cadillac on the lbj ranch

you know he used to do his business
in the oval office with the door open
negotiating votes
trousers around ankles
it was the sixties then
nobody dared light a match

mesas give way
to the bottom of the ocean
I'll need an ice cream
sandwich to make change

I'm drunk when band girlfriend arrives
i trade out my audience membership
knit highways in a manner
that made sense sober
how I found this hangover
is assumed but still unknown.

Civic Arena March 7 1984

snow on the dash
snow crunches under the tires
of a 77 rabbit, her friend's boyfriend
with a handful of pills to share
she plastered a pint in her jeans
security never looked anyway

into the dark of the floor
fog machine smells
the pills slowing down
speeding up together
diamond dave glitter blur
and fuzz this far away

running with the devil
into eruption, she never cared
for long solos but
whiskey and counting
23 times for the word jump
it's infinity…what's infinity?

drunk enough, on her boyfriends
shoulders, arms up gigantic
as they tore in
ain't talking 'bout love
last song and it's everything
spinning, freedom is ghost

waiting to go numb
the post office ain't the same
there ain't nothing wild
left of what remains.

Only Love Can Break Your Heart

when you're young and on your own
not that young
drunk, howling deep in the maryland night
trying to get the poison out of the soul
while poisoning the body

four am everything is alive
the alcohol kicked in
you want this to last and last and last
instead, you kick a few hours' sleep
before the hangover sun make its move
then richmond, fucking richmond
you sick southern belle
always waiting for me
to make a bloodshot fool of myself

truck stop speed, hair of the dog
makes everything right
then blues in the maryland night
she shines through small crowds
red hair, blue eyes follow
your hands as they strum
d minor to a seven following
the g around to the chorus

after a few songs
she waits in your coat
you follow her to her dorm
she wishes you were there all the time

a college girl's statement to college boys
it's clear your being placated

it doesn't change ceremony
the struggle to wring beauty from night
our ghost's, dream lovers
who turn to stars
to arrows in clasped hands
if you don't find what you want
at least your get what you need

she asks as the sun
comes apparent
would you like to get high?
slides from bed into panties
moves to the desk
meticulous with makings
sparks
returns
crawls into my chest

smoke hits lungs
I see the tragedy of her future
run across her eyes
I see every mile
annapolis to philly
run through my head
thin snow crust
makes tracks
covers tracks
I never need to be tethered
to any place again.

Road Trip to Winter Haven by Boxscore Junkies, 1979

We're Apollo 13 lucky out of Richmond.
We crawl in the Maverick sedan
past eighteen wheelers tipped on their sides.
We see a trooper's flashes through whiteout
by sawdust on an icy bridge as dangerous
as oil spilled under rubbers. We breathe deeply
by ugly Jacksonville's road dusted palm trees;
after fifteen merciless hours, ice melts
off the hood like we just left a carwash.
We walk into a 7-Eleven for snacks and pop
like dazed astronauts who kiss the ground
after splashing into the Pacific.

Sunbather at Round Hill Beach, 1973

"I won't go in
after the 4th,"
she said, reading
a dime store novel
on the sand.
She spies the shallows
between shoreline
and greased bodies
bobbing up
like seals.

Wiser Than Clocks

The foot of the bed
kicks you out.
Bank stocks drop
like meteorites.
You save soiled pennies
that sit in the safe
deposit coffin.
Gather the children but
brace yourself for antics
on the beaten, potholed roads.
You and she, a couple,
break apart
like a string of pearls.
Her rouged cheeks
aren't your nemesis,
aren't kitsch like pink
flamingos, and cosmetic
yard sale jewelry.
Harsher winds
search you out alone;
whip you
like a torn, festival flag.

LUKE KUZMISH

Jersey Poet
after Damian Rucci

a jersey poet
says you know you've got the audience
when someone wants to stab you in the gut
just for doing your job

bleed black onto shag carpet
with cigarette ashes, domestic beer,
someone's phony service dog,
and the woe of hopeful poets
         dying to become like the older poets
who don't bother with hope at all

he says let the girl from
a hippie van commune
sew your wounds shut
with her shoelaces

chicks love a scar and a good story
or a bad story if you tell it well.

Searching for You On Skellie Street

your cousin told me you were
living on Skellie Street
just a few blocks from our home

remember when we were kids? you would walk thru tall
      grass with a Squier bass in a 1970s Fender case
    to do our best with the elementary,
           Kurt Cobain and Neil Young
       orange stomp box, yellow cassette deck,
   black spaghetti of guitar cables
   on a bed of mashed
      grey shag

maybe I'd see you, I told your cousin,
walking my boy in the stroller
no specific plans because I knew
running into you might mean
awkward conversations and undead hurt
the divergence of boyhood best
friends who drift
apart, into men

Saturday morning feeling brave
I walked the length of Skellie Street
from its gentle bending origins
looking for the house where you
    drink to beckoning dreams,

drink to resolve death:
Bobby's foreclosed potential,
West Virginian suicide,
the leather of your grandfather's face

drink to wash away
        the taste of cigarettes

drink
        just to drink

maybe I was feeling brave knowing
you'd be sleeping off a hangover
or pruning branches off an antique tree
in the blue dawn of heaven
so I wouldn't have to think
        about what you might think about me,
        how time can feel like a betrayal
searching for you on Skellie Street
        I came up empty handed

I couldn't find a facade
that matched what I could remember about you
        no waving flag of 80s hair band
        no solemn memorial to Tom Petty
        no 12-string guitar resting in the gutter
                its smooth finish a bed for dead leaves
no wounded heart counting falling stars.

Just To Not Feel Useless

I wiped the saliva from your chin
just to not feel useless

a coma,
intubated
in miserable pajamas
with another attempt

the sunlight dying
thru the lonely windows
of those
who beckon the bull
with the red of their hearts

still haven't learned
how to knock on death's door
or what to say
when death answers.

JOHN A. CLAYTON

Riddle of Life

I know who I am, but not many do.
You see what I want, as I am sure you do too.
I know that I see only your outside skin.
It is only in our hearts that we hide our sins.

Only you can know what is in your heart of hearts.
Only with great effort can you even start
to ask yourself questions that bruise the soul.
The hardest questions that leave you cold.

Searching one's soul, an exercise only you can do.
It may hurt but it's good for you.
How could I have not known the words were cruel?
Words, like a hammer, are also a tool.

It's easy to blame others and not look at you.
Just look in the mirror. Look carefully and you can see too.
What everyone else sees is really not you.
The kernel of your being can only be seen by a perceptive few.

The Home Place

The old clay bricks of the chimney blend in with the rusty brown roof. On sunny afternoons Turkey Vultures like to perch on the peak because it is easy to hitch a ride on the breeze coming up the hollow. The exhausted Goldenrod glisten silver in the Autumn sun and hide the shallow well where a family of twelve got water for cooking and cleaning, except in August when the well would go dry and water had to be carried up the hill from the spring. The old house only has two rooms and a leanto on the East side. The doors have rotted off but the green roll roofing on the sides has held up pretty good. Between the house and barn is the garden spot. It went a long way toward feeding all those kids and among the rocks, the dirt is still black.Mom and Dad died years ago and at least 3 or 4 of the kids have passed too. All the kids grew up and got the hell out of Dodge. There was nothing here for them on this hardscrabble farm, where the soil is thin and rock ledges run right to the surface and blink in the daylight. Like most Ozark young'ins, they left Maries County seeking fame and fortune in other places. For years they were all gone. They have started drifting back in, some with pensions earned in more progressive places and others with not much more than Social Security. At least it's cheaper to live here than most places. There's nobody left that gives a damn about this old place, except maybe me, and I didn't even grow up here.

Columbia Regional Airport

Waiting for the arrival of Flight U A 5840 from Chicago,
I remembered when I was 17 and this land was just
a soybean field surrounded by brush piles and Multiflora Rose.
Out the East window of the Berkshire House, I watched
the coyotes worry the brush pile.

The pressure on the rabbit to run, mounted.
I wondered if uncertainty and fear would cause
it to abandon caution and make a run for it.
Run? But to where? Just another brush pile
or clump of Multiflora Rose? So another
cycle of intimation and fear could begin?
The largest coyote jumped on top of the brush pile
and began digging and yelping.
Could the coyote reach the rabbit by scratching at the limbs?
Who knows? Terror is a great motivator.
Too much for the rabbit! It raced out of the brush pile
and had a thirty yard head start before the coyotes knew it was gone.
The race was on! 200 yards to the bank of the creek.
The coyotes were gaining.
Out of nowhere, a shadow over head, talons reached forward,
the rabbit screamed and was airborne.
The coyotes stopped running, milled around looking puzzled,
as they watched their almost meal disappear
into the wild blue yonder.
The rabbit was erased by something it did not see coming.
There are no more soy beans, no more brush piles,
no more Multiflora Rose, no more rabbits.

Only concrete, chain-link fences, stone and metal buildings,
cars, airplanes. The only sounds are the sounds of cars,
a loud speaker no one can understand,
the squawk of rubber hitting runway,
the whir of automatic sliding doors.
The only animal life are little dogs
wearing colorful clothing, tugging at
leashes held by old women.
All the humans wear faces pinched with anxiety
and uncertainty. Wondering if today is the day
they will be erased by something they can not see coming.

JASON MAYER

Dyslexia

When people hear dyslexia
They think reading disorder
Backwards words
Mixed up sentences
Scrambled numbers
I wish it was that simple
Reading problems are there
But they are a symptom
The real problem is all in my head
No really
It's literally all in my head
Swimming letters
Jumbled numbers
Shifting sentences
Every sound in range
Every visual distraction
It's all in my head
Always in my head
Conversations from the right
Appear on my left
A table full of people
Becomes a cloud of confusion
Too many voices
Too many conversations
Processing slows to half speed
Vertigo kicks in
I feel dizzy
Not sick

But cloudy
Like a London fog
Objects appear
Then disappear
Sounds muddle together
Eye contact is crucial
Connecting sounds to subjects
Next is tunnel vision
A defensive reaction
It helps to center me
But dulls the senses
I'm forced to concentrate
One conversation at a time
Working hard not to let it show
Smile for the people
Focus on fixed objects
Deep breaths
I close my eyes for a second
Rubbing them for camouflage
I tell people I have mild dyslexia
I don't know why
I don't even know what that means
It makes me feel better
Less weak
Less damaged
Less mentally ill
It's like telling people
I have a mild peg leg
It's still a peg leg
Sure I can walk on it
It may be shorter than others
Less debilitating than others

More hidden than others
But it is still a wooden leg
As a child
It was a reading problem
Comprehension problem
Spelling problem
Behavioral problem
Leading to assessments
Then evaluations
And finally the dreaded labels
As a teenager
It was an embarrassment
No one wants to be labeled
Labeled with a disorder
Labeled with a mental illness
Labeled as slow
Labeled as less than
As an adult
It's a mild inconvenience
Molded to be mild
After years of treatment
Hours of reading lessons
Pages of writing exercises
Auditory exercises
Breathing exercises
Focusing exercises
Fine motor activities
Word building activities
Memory building activities
The never ending therapy sessions
Each containing new terms
Phoneme segmentation

Phonological awareness
Sing-song reading
Eye-text tracking
Visual processing improvement
Syllable substitution
Syllable stretching
Syllable segmentation
Letter reversal
Letter inversion
Word substitution
Word transposition
Word reversal
They are part of me now
Along with my dyslexia
I have assimilated them
They are a part of me now
Along with my dyslexia
I cling to those mechanisms
Like a warm blanket
When the fog comes
When the letters swim
When the numbers tangle
When the sounds mix
When the confusion sets in
I find solace in those mechanisms
I have assimilated them
They are a part of me now
Along with my dyslexia.

A Good Man

What Does it Mean to Be a Man?
According to biology I have all the right parts.
The size,
The shape,
The dangly bits.
These thing are anatomically correct,
But do they make me a man?
Or merely define me as male?

The TV commercials tell me that I'm a man,
Though I'm not as cool as the guys in those ads.
Am I a man because of what I drink?
Because of what I eat?
What I smell like?
What I look like?
Because I drive a manly truck?
Do these things make me a man?
That would be way too easy.

My grandpa said I became a man when I joined the Marines.
But I am not the hero that he was.
Am I a man because I won a couple fights?
Shot a bunch of weapons?
Threw a few grenades?
Watched brave men die?
Did harm to my enemies?
Is this really what it takes be a man?
I'm not so sure.

My father said I became a man when I got married.
But I think he was just being supportive.
Am I a man because I got married in uniform?
Cut the cake with a sword?
Removed my bride's garter with my teeth?
Maybe it's because I married better than my station,
But that just means my wife is a good woman.

My Muslim friend said I became a man when I fathered a son.
He calls me Abunoah, father of Noah.
Am I a man because of my seed?
Because of my Y chromosome?
Because I smoked a cigar at the birth of a son?
Because the coin flip of fate landed on boy versus girl?
Maybe I'm missing something,
But I believe my friend is wrong about this one.

My professor once called me a man among boys.
It made feel equal parts proud and embarrassed.
Am I a man because I earned a degree?
Was it the bachelors?
The masters?
Or the Ph. D?
I believe that just makes me a doctor,
But it has little to do with me being a man.

An Elder at my church once called me a good man,
But I feel small standing next to my mentors.
Am I a man because of what I believe?
Who I believe in?

How many services I attend?
These things make me a Christian,
But they are not unique to being a man.

My wife calls me the man of the house,
But after 25 years of marriage what else could she say.
Am I a man because I bring home the bacon?
Keep the yard mowed?
Help with the dishes?
Bought a few roses?
These things are important,
But I'm not sure they define me as a man.

My old boss called me a hard working man.
Probably because I helped make him rich.
Am I a man because I worked long hours?
Held fancy titles?

Earned more money?
Started my own business?
I'm proud of those things, but not because I'm a man?
It's just not that simple.

Maybe I'll never understand what it truly means to be a man.
All I can do is try my best,
To be loving,
To be good,
To be kind,
Faithful,
Gentle,

Peaceful,
Tolerant,
Joyful,
And self-controlled.
If I can do this more often than not,
Then maybe, in the end,
They will say, "He was a good man."

The Utter Destruction

I believe in fire
The white hot flames
The blistering heat
The raging infernos
The utter destruction

I believe in air
The harsh winds
The massive gusts
The turning vortexes
The utter destruction

I believe in water
The crashing waves
The darkest depths
The suffocating pressure
The utter destruction

I believe in earth
The muddy slides
The falling rocks
The exploding volcanoes
The utter destruction

I believe in love
The unrequited feelings

The broken hearts
The shattered homes
The utter destruction

I believe in all these things
And their utter destruction.

STEVE BRISENDINE

Phantom

Streetlights
pass through me now;
so, too, strangers' glances,
the night-winds of
almost-spring.
I am a muffled chime,
bells wrapped in glass wool;

a crystal kaleidoscope filled
with shards of champagne flutes,
the dust of diamonds.
I am an echo of cat-feet
and Bradbury whispers
down streets where lovers walk,
dance in shadows,
dream themselves ghosts.
Crows no longer flap
and caw when I pass.
Their flat black eyes
can see the dead, but they do not
fear me.

Tongues of Flame in The House of God

I: the cloud by day
only some of the
smoke rises up to Heaven,
a grim billow of
red-letter King James *thees* and
thous and *thines*, of cabinets
and chairs and crayon

portraits of the Twelve; the rest
spills northwest, low to
the ground, shrouds my way (breathe in
Alpha, breathe out *Omega*)

II: the fire by night
neighbor-strangers line
Reeds Road, watch from upwind as
flames refuse to die;
we speculate cost and cause,

swap variations on a
theme of *I heard the*
helicopter, then sirens,
but I never smelled
any smoke (at home, dinner
is waiting, slowly burning)

Shine and Show

All that
we can do, we
who call ourselves poets,
is to carefully curate the
remains

of love,
of pain, of moments in their most
timeless forms, and put them
on display; sign
your name

upon
the paper, if
you must, but know this much:
that which you claim to own *(This is
my tongue,*

my hand,
my idea and no one else's)
is but held in common –
all the world's words
in yours.

Quintessence

The green, green earth orbits and spins in unison with the ocean's tides.
Pausing for a moment, perceiving that the wide rolling waves are
boundless.
Each ripple absorbed by a fathomless blue, tossing, bubbling, and surging,
A progression connecting balmy breeze and water, body and soul,
ebb, and flow.
Sand can lie silent and still, but with pressure from the ever-pounding
surf, granules may form a mold, a temporary work of art, a soft
inlay, a subtle slope.
Winds and waves press on all day and play their role in this display.
We need the ocean and wind and sand to teach us and shape us.
We are separate, but we are one planet, in rooms connected by salt
and sea.

The Farm

The still, spacious kitchen at the farm,
before the room filled with bright, bright sunlight.
Voices before the gathering of belly warmed chicken eggs,
and bowls of cereal,
and warm, fruity kuchens.
The small, top drawer filled with pennies,
and nickels, and dimes.
It smelled of gum, minty and sweet.
The floor in the utility room is cool.
The stone shaped tiles fit together
like a large sepia shaded puzzle.
I imagined the shapes were countries,
or boots, or spaces to play hopscotch on.
The floor was strong, and its integrity
lasted long after the farm was abandoned.

Moirai

A pink dawn lingers as she makes her way to the beach.
Tracing feather-like patterns of mice and snails in the wet sand
    with her toes,
wind blows over the ocean waves.
Pausing long enough to become aware of the warm water
    washing first her ankles,
then her knees,
her feet reach for something solid underneath.
With each wave she perceives a certain balance.
And with each wave,
more and more space washes away beneath her.
Her arms float,
as if suspended by strings – threads attached to soft stars.
Seagulls circle with their curious heads cocked to the side.
Soon they could be tangled in her floating hair.
The distant horizon is dark violet.
She breathes deeply of the salty air,
and tastes the ocean.
The shore becomes a life path,
And she follows.

PAUL KONIECKI

By the Near-dark Pillows
Night Meant Love

the iris of your eye
looks like the surface
of a planet where i

have been but
i have never been
without you

a finger of light
breaks the flat dark
line of yesterday's horizon

i think of you saying
time is another kind of
choice

we can't have
a partial avalanche
or a little bit of

waterfall to drink
i double check
you've taken

your medicine
and roll back
over like a leaf

on a hill
the house plant mentions
to the window shade

the morning is coming
the moon is done
baby baby

shut your eyes
make a spoon
listen

to the sheets whisper
the proper way
to make a bed up all along.

A Dream Covid is Over and We're in Jersey
or Missouri Making a Show

For Damian

You are opening a box with a cutter
And your lungs with a cigarette

A bus passes
The band is in the back warming up

Cap it off like a well-fire
You tell a coworker when they ask

What to do about their soon to be
Latest crazy ex

I'm trying to read your directions
To tonight's venue

Rebecca is hurrying over
Your cheetah-print dress

Last week purpose
Appeared to me

As cupid sent to kill love with a bow
Or evangelicals christ

To teach me how to choke pain
Off at its source

This is our first show as co-hosts
There must be one place

Everything begins
One fountain one fissure

One crack in the fabric pulsing
Like the best wounds throb

Tonight is a river
And a bell.

Legend of the Lightning Flies

Beginning
As a cage of wire
The sun rang out
To the end of ends
Like a broken bell

Icecaps gone
The once mighty Atlantic
Reduced to foam
In a song about seas

From the bridge
Eyelashes try
To anoint
Lightning flies

Burn flags
And still
Storms advance
If only we

Painted
The White
House Black
Before it slid
To New Orleans

Where people are alone
When counts for less
Through window glass
Birds flutter in your smile

This is how we
Die our own net
Held breath and
Suffocation let it un-be

Like Goonies
Lightning Flies
Consort with pirates
And never say die.

Strip-mining Rumi at 2 a.m.

There's four lights on the radio tower
behind Morgan's, five if you count the
flashing white one.

I don't count the white one, because on
the inside i'm red; so i only count the
four red ones.

I can hear the rippling air from each
transmission, like an echo of ghosts;

we all got voices somewhere.

My love is…

My love is a fragile flower
Packing an M-16
& grenade launcher.
My love is an ice-sickle
Showing the slow drip
In bathroom
How to form solidly.
My love is a vacuum that
Consumes everything in
Its path until the next
Morning is nothing more
Than a puddle of vomited
Memories.
My love is amnesia.

Ode to Jeffers__

It's the reverse world, the inverse of things
that collides with the projection of
ideology.

Staring out stone windows, his mind felt like
a bonfire; sweat beaded down his jaw line.

Everything about the shards of perception
that cut across the mind like diamonds
he could not reconcile with speech.

Bitter sweet mirrors and endless cups of
coffee fuel the tension of thought
as he climbs out onto the high wire.

Thumbing his way back to source.

Clouds

She remembers a time
when things mattered,
when everything wasn't
always gone.

Time and days,
people and their plans,
all of this made sense,
had a place
in the collective everything.
She flips back through
old calendars
trying to pinpoint exactly
when it all turned
and became this
grey mist of a life.

She wonders if it's a
chemical imbalance,
or maybe it's the
rest of the world.

She remembers those colors;
they were so vivid,
so shockingly bright
they could blind a person

if they weren't ready,
or at least
shake them to tears.

Everything smelled like life,
everything flowed,
moved with easy purpose.
She sees the children
on the playground
outside her bedroom window,
hears the beautiful cries,
the warmth in each movement.
She sees the sun
just above the clouds.

Calling

She finds the things that
no one wants
to often be things of beauty.

Rusted-out drive shafts in a ditch,
spent cigarette butts in an alley,
over ripened fruit on the ground
beside the overflowing dumpster.

She once found a discarded mic stand,
the spring-loaded clip at the top
no longer springy,
and with no leap of faith,
with no forceful synapse magic,
she saw the magnificence,
took it home,
and let it begin.

As a sculptor has only to
release the art imprisoned
within the marble,
she's only to let the detritus of society
speak to her.

It always does,
and she always listens.

On frenetic, electric late nights,
she wonders why
the rest of the world
can't hear the scream.

The Factory

She comes here
when there's nothing else.

Those first
tentative steps
not so long ago,
when everything was dark,
the rain was freezing,
and the gravel surrounding
shifted with every step,
threatening to be like all the rest;
to try it's damnedest
to take her down.

She found this place
on a bright, cold day,
but it is at night
when she chooses to visit.
Not every night;
only when she needs it,
and lucky enough;
we need it to.

There is love in this place,
and she doesn't have to look far
beyond the cracked bare concrete floors,
the exposed wiring

that saw its last spark
long ago,
the scant traces of things
that've come here for refuge,
and never left.

M.J. Arcangelini

Bobcat

Under an
orange sun
bobcat drinks
from water
set out for deer
stalks a squirrel
across the yard
chases it halfway
up an oak tree
then changes his
mind and turns
around to climb
down head first
sits at the base
unsatisfied
still hungry for
blood and meat
the hunt and kill
while the squirrel
twitters on its
rocking branch
surviving for
one more day
of gathering
ripe acorns
and waiting
for rain.

Hummingbird At The Bottlebrush

How do a hummingbird's wings
sound to the hummingbird?

Are they so loud that they drown
out the other sounds of the world?

Or does the hummingbird not
even hear them anymore, the

way a man grows accustomed
to the constant tinnitus of these

complicated times and learns to
hear only what he wants to hear.

My Father Goes To Florida (1978)

Midsummer on a Florida beach, wading into the moonlit glow of
the Atlantic, water erupts with leaping fish, shimmering shark food.

In the cardio ICU my father, hooked up to tubes and wires, sees me
enter and quietly starts to cry, realizing the family has been called.

He tells me he loves me and it is the only time I can remember
him ever saying those words; I don't know how to respond.

In the RV park insects hum in the darkness, televisions
mumble incoherently within mobile replications of home.

The only other time I saw my father cry was 1964. I was 11.
He was on the phone. Someone told him that his father died.

In a phone booth on a night muggier than Ohio a rainbow scarab
appeared, nearly as large as a praying mantis; metallic reflections.

MICHAEL H. BROWNSTEIN

The Aftermath

after a visit to the Pine Ridge Reservation, South Dakota

I woke badly this morning
flesh of cucumbers piled on the kitchen counter
the dogs resting behind their barricade
outside, a Monsanto gray

the snare drum still needs a resting place
two cardboard boxes outside the door rust
a splinter of glycerin in my palm
a running field with a keep off sign
green leaves oil dark

some days the sun misses the point
Pine Ridge gathers itself in shadow and pollutants
yesterday no one marched.

Silence is Often the Loudest of Sounds

In the night of the rust moon,
a thin glaze surrounds it,
opaque, translucent,
the frayed edges of silk,
as if it were a shroud
light as the powder on the monarch's wings.

We settle into the darkness of silence,
let the shadows merge,
and when one of us speaks,
sound breaks into water.
The moon drops its light on everything,
the trees and brush grow distinct,

but its shroud grows longer,
a soft fog falling over it.
The vernacular of moonlit skies
touches us, the things around us,
and as the clouds of night fall to earth,
it remains dragon eyed bloodshot red.

Parameters

She is a pond,
a boulder slides down the mountainside
hitting the water with a clash of chaos,
not ripples of circles
but a churning of essence.

She is a pond
a rock slides down the mountainside
hitting the water with great greed,
not ripples of circles
but a twisting of essence.

She is a pond,
a pebble slides down the mountainside
hitting the water with a soul of song,
and, yes, ripples into circles
a definition of essence.

She sleeps in the dreams of others.

Awake, she is the boulder,
then the rock,
and as she touches the cold floor,
a small pebble.

If only a dream could have a beginning, middle and end.

The pond fills itself with melting snow,
fallen leaf,
erosion and stone.

Wind prays over it,
animals drink of it,
fish somehow thrive within it.

She feels the pond within her,
its water her blood,
its lifeforce her muscles, her heartbeat.

Trees shade it on one side.
Large formations block another.
A boulder cannot make it through.

She does not know the strangers in her dreams.

The hike to the pond is steep,
the trail carved out of rock and earth,
tree limb and a faltering of light.

It is not easy to find
nor is it easy to reach,
but she does, bends for a drink, and for no reason sings.

And when she lays her head down to nap,
she finds the psalms of others,
their wishes and desires,
their hopes and their triumphs,
every dream a segment of essence,
of scent,
a need to dream strong.

ARTURO MANTECON

ALFONSO, ALFONSO...

Sometimes it was hard to fall asleep. I would lie in bed, smothering on the inchoate fears that would weigh upon my chest with the descending dark. I would keep my eyes shut out of dread of seeing the brutish imps that perched upon and clung to the headboard, waiting for me to lose consciousness. Sharp-taloned, long-armed, fiendish creatures hid and lurked obscure in my room that had become vast and unfamiliar with the night.

Sometimes it was hard to fall asleep.

It did not help matters that, just the year before, the Bikini atoll had been obliterated by a hydrogen bomb, a test blast that swept away a mothball fleet of battleships assembled around that Pacific reef, swept them away like so many fragile toy boats, the film of the incomprehensible explosion shown over and over on television, so that the vision of horror would remain precise and retinal even with both eyes shut.

It did not help matters that the nuns of St. Theresa's parochial school informed us second graders that Detroit would be among the very first American cities bombed in an atomic war.

The nuns of St. Theresa's parochial school assured us second graders that we could protect ourselves, if it so happened that the godless Russians dropped on H-bomb on our city, by crouching and cowering under our wood and cast-iron desks and covering our heads with arms and hands.

Sometimes it was hard to fall asleep.

I would lay there in the dark, and the deep droning crescendo of the propellers of every passing passenger plane would convince me that it was the implacable minions of Nikita flying overhead to loosen death from the unseen skies.

Sometimes it was hard to fall asleep, and when my anxiety became too oppressive, I would call out to my father.

He never failed to come. The door would open and admit the light and admit my father into my room... the most confident, haphazard man the world has ever seen, dressed always in white shirt and tie, flourishing a whistling rendition of the Atcheson, Topeka, and the Santa Fe or Flat Foot Floogie or some other Slim Gaillard tune...looking a dark composite of Jack Webb and Walter Matthau...

"And what can I do for you?"

"It's hard for me to fall asleep. Tell me a story, dad."

"A story? One story coming right up!"

And he would sit on my bed and lean his head back against the headboard, smelling of Old Spice and cigars and would tell me a story, always the same story, invariable in every detail.

"I'll tell you a story about my days in the Army, m'hijo...I was in the Army and we made camp for the night, and

we gathered 'round the fire, and my captain said to me, 'Alfonso, Alfonso, please tell us a story'.

So I told my captain this story: I was in the Army and we made camp for the night, and we gathered 'round the fire, and my captain said to me, 'Alfonso, Alfonso, please tell us a story'.

So I told my captain this story: I was in the Army and we made camp for the night, and we gathered 'round the fire, and my captain said to me, 'Alfonso, Alfonso, please tell us a story'.

So I told my captain this story: I was in the Army and we made camp for the night, and we gathered 'round the fire, and my captain said to me, 'Alfonso, Alfonso, please tell us a story...'"

And on and on my father would continue with his story of a weird train of Alfonsos telling their stories, stories verbatim of every preceding one, until I could keep my eyes open no longer and until my mind lost its hold on the skein of the yarn, and I lapsed into sleep like one overwhelmed by too many sheep.

Over the next several years, this was a common occurrence...this bedtime story telling of my father's...the story never changing, the results always the same...and with every telling of the story, by this everyday man who was my father, the mystery and power of it was magnified until it seemed as though it could subordinate and engulf the entirety of the world and all in it.

"Alfonso, Alfonso, please tell us a story," and I would find myself present at the fire with the fatigue-clad soldiers, their faces lit by the flames and waiting for Alfonso to tell them a tale. My father's voice would issue from Alfonso's mouth, and I would step toward the fire into the presence of another fire at another camp with the same soldiers listening to their captain plead for a story and another father-voiced Alfonso would begin to speak, and I would go to the fire again to enter another self-same camp with identical soldiers and a captain and Alfonso and, "Alfonso, Alfonso, please tell us a story."

And I was pulled by my father's voice and drawn to campfire after campfire, traveling headlong into my father's story of a story of a story until it seemed that I was opening boxes within boxes within boxes, or that I was discovering nested dolls within dolls, like those Russian lacquered dolls called "matrioshka", each babushka-headed doll apparently identical to another doll contained within it, just as each story was identical in scope and space and time to the story contained within it.

"Alfonso, Alfonso, please tell us a story."

And I would open and enter each box of a story, and I seemed unchanged in self-perceived size, but of logical necessity I became smaller, as I stepped into each sequentially smaller box of place, time, words, and deeds, the total singularity of the story itself getting larger and larger, bigger and bigger, as I entered deeper and deeper within it, the historical margins of the story farther and farther off, farther and farther away in an immensity of smallness, in a dynamic immensity of permanent dimension.

"Alfonso, Alfonso, please tell us a story."

And the story was like opposing mirrors reflecting each other in a blind symmetry and affording a view of a receding infinity inviting an intrepid Alice to enter and enter and enter a teleidoscopic universe of microcosmic enormity, which, once entered, is inescapable, which, once entered, leads to galaxies of forgetfulness and the realization of the atomic repetition of all that has ever been or will be, a story that is the monad and aleph of the Logos.

And I cannot help but imagine that, somewhere on the outer edge of connectedness, where the sinews of immeasurable story are stretched until the smooth impervious membranes of time become networked and permissive of alternate events, that there could be other, different stories told by Alfonso or perhaps even told by Mohammed or Nadia or Jennie, stories told by each of the soldiers at the campfire, stories of consequence, stories

of little import, stories nonsensical, nothing mattering but the stories, stories intersecting and reflecting and ignorant of each other in a spherical geometry of ecstatic words in a universe of infinite axes that the irresistible, all-devouring stories make small, finite, profane, and inscrutable.

"Alfonso, Alfonso, please tell us a story."

I, unlike some small children, never believed that my father held the keys to any sort of wisdom. Some children see their fathers as heroic and omniscient beings; I did not.

As a matter of fact, I didn't think my father knew anything at all, not anything, that is, that mattered. All my father knew was the world of praxis. I saw mystery all about me. For my father, the world held no mysteries.   How could my father lift the veil of illusion and struggle with the chaotic magic behind it if he did not, could not, see the veil at all?

It didn't even occur to me…it would never have occurred to me… that he could explain even those mysteries which he himself created.

So I never thought to ask him why he told me the same story every single time, every single night. There was but the night, my fear, the story, and I would not ask him why.

So I never thought to ask him why he referred to the Alfonso of the story in the first person singular. My father's name was not even Alfonso. There was but the night, my fear, the story, and I would not ask him why.

Each night of the story I would call for him, and I would hear his heavy wing-tipped footfall in the hallway. The amber light would reclaim my room for me, and there he would be: the white shirt, dark tie, the clothes he would wear on the job at Epps' Sporting Goods. There was his incomparable whistling joy. He would recline on the bed,

his weight and mass creating a strong gravitational pull that would attract my smaller body, like a large celestial body bending space itself. There was the story each night, each time. His story. I asked for nothing more, expected nothing more. There was but the night, my fear, the story, and I would not ask him why.

I never told my father of all the thoughts birthed in my head by his idiotic, redundant story.

I never told him how much its staggering, complexity confounded me and amazed me.

The story may not have been my father's. The story may have been told to him when a boy. The story may have been a family heirloom. The story may have been a confused conundrum put in his mouth by a frustrated god.

I never asked my father what his intentions were. I never asked him whether the story was meant to be didactic. I never asked him whether it was meant to amuse. I never asked him whether it was meant to annoy. I never asked him whether it's only purpose was to put me to sleep and make me dream. I never asked him why he never asked me why I never asked him any of these things.

I never asked my father a thousand things. What he never told me was all I ever needed.

ALEXIS RHONE FANCHER

Double-Timed at the Nickel Diner

—for Clare

Tanya raised the Coke to her lips. Took a swig. Mouthed the words: *Wanna get outta here, baby?* I watched as she rammed her tongue into the bottle for emphasis, her blue eyes fixed on my brown ones. No mistaking that, I thought. I'd waited all my life for a girl like Tanya, wild as the wind. The girl my mama warned me about. My best friend's girl. Terry was sitting right next to her, for chrissake! And she, acting like he wasn't. Tanya had a habit of sucking her left thumb. An oral fixation, always something in her mouth. In my dreams, my cock was in her mouth; I'd wake up sticky and spent. Now she was making noises like she wanted me for real, and I admit, I felt qualmish. I was raised better. And Terry? He was like a brother. But that girl had me by the balls, mesmerized. Her long, dark hair, framing her face, flowing past her tits, fragrant, like night blooming jasmine. *Hey, Terry*, I said, to break Tanya's spell. "Wadya wanna do now?" Terry shrugged, intent on finishing his burger. Idiot. Never could see what was right in front of him. I watched him chew. Tanya watched the clock on the diner's wall. "Tick tock. Tick tock," she said.

Published in *MacQueen's Quinterly*, Fall, 2020.

Sex, Guns, and the Canadians Next Door

A big caliber bullet goes in like a dime and comes out like a cash register, M says. His gun is out of the case. He fancies himself a thrill killer. Or a poet. It's August. Muggy. The air in the apartment so thick, M's innuendo can't reach me. Across the alley, the Canadian couple are at it again; wild fucking with the drapes wide and lights on, a tutorial for us less fortunates. He's a big man, hulking, and she, a sweet blonde with multiple piercings, straddles him like a horse. They're smooth-skinned. Athletic. These days, all I do is watch. Me and M, we don't fuck like that anymore; a girl slips up just one time, and it's the permanent cold shoulder. Like he was such an angel? *That's different,* he says. *Sorry,* I don't say again. Instead, I stare across the alley into my neighbors' lives. I'm naked, the way M likes me (but for those black kitten heels he wants me to wear), and I play with myself while he plays with his gun, just out of frame. I'm hoping he'll get the message, that I'm horny enough to make it up to him and try again, or just rut, no strings, but he's consumed with a different kind of gun, his big-bulleted, Smith & Wesson .38. Massages it with linseed oil, ramrods the barrel.

Published in *EROTIC: New & Selected*, NYQ 2021

(Three Little Words)

for Francesca Bell

1.

M has never said I *love* you before.
Not to me.

2.

He cries at weddings, like a girl.

3.

The sex is only good if we're totally fucked up.
It blurs how wrong we are for each other.

4.

English is not M's native tongue. It eludes him.

5.

Maybe he misspoke?
His prepositions hang mid-air.

He says it's hard to think when it's hard.

6.

M's white teeth nibble at my clit like a ferret.
The two front ones indent slightly;
it makes him look goofy, like a joke.

Sometimes when we have sex, M's calico meow trips
across my back. Rakes a claw. Caterwauls.

She doesn't want me here.

Sometimes when we have sex, I am the one in heat.

7.

Outside, the tin roof rain suicides
on the hard-packed earth.

M is fucking me from behind,
his body melded into my ass,
fingers kneading my breasts.
He's mumbling up the courage.
I know what he's trying to say.
I want to fuck him mute.

8.

In the bedroom there's this
Dennis Hopper photo of Tuesday Weld,
driving, top down, blonde hair streaming.
Circa 1968. She's unfettered.

Why can't he see that
I am that girl, *my* top down,
my hair streaming,
my consequence-less life?

9.

M. bought the print for me but
I don't want it.

I want nothing from him but
a silent film, a carnival.
I want him to want that, too.

I want him to shut up but
he zeros in on my ear

and says it.

First Published in *Cactus Heart Magazine,* 2014.

JOHN MACKER

Cerrado

Listening to Mingus' *Gunslinger Bird*
in the living room when I heard a loud thump
coming from her studio. She was on the floor
holding her bent Quasimodo wrist. As ugly a
break as I'd ever been to. She had slipped and
landed on her hip and hand. She went briefly
into shock and stared at the ceiling.
She didn't recognize me as her husband
thought I was playing live music from somewhere
in the Five Points of her imagination. After she
came around she swore the darkness tried to
close in around her. I took her to urgent care
on a hot smoky night, the drowse of August.
They determined she'd need surgery. They
determined older people slip and fall, right
before we begin to fade away.
We are too old to be gunslingers. Bird died at 34.
The nights closed in on him like carnivorous angels.

She now holds her bandaged wrist above her heart
and walks with a cane. Life doesn't feel precious, it
resembles an open wound we spend a lot of our time closing.
Wildfire smoke fills the air, the sun has turned orange.
Another man of color shot in the back.
Who doesn't want to close the book on this grievous year?
Who hasn't gone into shock, eyes filled with ash?

Today, I played music so loud it emptied the neighborhood
of life as we know it. But it gradually returned.
The silent ambulance mercifully left the cul-de-sac
without the sick lady across the street. Victor brought
in his recycling bin. I read: *some words die in cages.*
I thought about what breaks us, what mends us, the border,
separations. What closes our hearts for good.
I thought about hair trigger America,
how smoke is the summer language of ghosts.

Whitman's Beard

It's too early for the joyous butterflies
of Whitman's grey beard. All that's left from
last summer in the yard are their spirit skins.
The lady across the street went into assisted living,
her ambulance has disappeared. The sirens have
alerted the dead to an uncertain afterlife. In his
eyes you can still see his words, his war, in
our eyes the sun's faux spring brightness.
March, if we listen to the gossip, will change
everything. It's been a long grey year and language has
softened the hard edge of isolation. At sunset,
a distracted horizon winks at the sky. In
isolation, we've opened our hearts to essential
pollinators, the drought will likely leave them
speechless. The indissoluble flowers will be
surly, their colors will cast shadows on our
defoliated lives. This summer
Lorca will lead us to the joyous butterflies
of Whitman's beard and we'll join him
and pray for rain.

Song

Under this blue basement
floor of the heavens
a moment in the world
I'll never relive:
    fastidious Cooper's hawk scans the yard

for a meal of mourning dove
parks his shadow
on the pine-needled ground
like a birthmark.
For a moment, winter

is led away in zip cuffs.
Song has crossed the border and
gone underground.
We share the common language
of held breaths.

SHAWN PAVEY

A Late Morning Gully Washer and
a Perfect Pot of Coffee

Let's stay inside and play
those Small Faces records maybe
some pre-Mtv J. Geils Band
Diamond Dogs era Bowie

                  some *Rebel Rebel*

          let's dance our hearts out in the gloom
            the floor is swept and we have the room

                    crank it up baby
play it loud and make those dishes in the kitchen cupboard clink
             baby make those glasses shake
       we can rattle the dust loose
and play that blues record
               you know the one
             Muddy Waters

oh darlin' that's it

I'll be your hoochie coochie man

                  better yet
          I'll be the man you need me to be

Epiphanies

Who knows anything about epiphanies anymore? We can't write epiphanies off our taxes. Profit and loss of this kind cannot be measured or entered in spreadsheets. No, epiphanies will bring pain. Or they are pain. Serendipity, now that's something. Sailing about on oceans willy-nilly looking for silk because where there is silk riches will soon follow. History tells us this but what does history know about silk, about empires rising and falling in silk. Dance is taxed and taxing and I should be discouraged from telling you about it because heavy as we are we all dance in tornadoes.

Channeling Ryberg

It might be after 3 a.m.
and sleep is a mystery
you've never uncracked
and you think of a sandwich
even though your
belt is a little more snug
these days and these days
you want to "avenge the death
of your master" but you can't remember
his or her or their name
not that it ever mattered anyway
so you listen to Son House
with the volume set low
as to not disturb the rest
of your wife who is safely employed
and keeping you from a homeless shelter
and you thank her quietly
and often for the save
and Son sings to you
Oh, the blues is a lowdown old aching chill
If you ain't had 'em boys, I- I hope you never will
but you have had and you do have
that coldness in your bones
that grind and creak and crack of bones
with each rising out of chairs.

ROB AZEVEDO

Gaging On Cold Cuts

same routine, same thoughts
most circling around a woman
with wide hips
or a bent hose-covered knee
or the dizzying hint of an areola
brazenly displayed in the cold cut aisle.

these thoughts, this routine,
fully encrusted, each of them,
fanged in spots with silver tips,
spouting words forgotten
by Kings and Queens.

these barren crusted thoughts
arrive steady as the evening news,
ridden upon the backs of
frauds and finks,
as the long eared beaters
cough and gag on the night
from the street outside my window.

these thoughts,
these thoughts,
these thoughts,
always circling the drain,
spiraling down in a cascade

of deliberate brutishness,
vain with gummed up wisdom,
constricted by need,
consumed with lust,
as these thoughts shop for eggs and bread
peering unseen into the blouses
of firm breasted strangers
standing over bargain meats,
measuring their might
against my own.

Lay Heavy On My Skin

A crushing glance
glowing beyond recognition
lays heavy on my skin
as piles of bent twisted rays
spring fast across
my hung dried neck
weathered pockets of gloom
abandoned by dabs of light
languishing on river beds
on mountainsides
on matted sands flooded with pennies
and rings of constellations
pairing peacefully
on the crystal shores
sliding sideways against
my hangdog grin.

Fogged Over

The glint in my eye fogs over
as the meat of my hands
begin to rumble.

The rustling started in my chest, that
rambling, hollow, slow rolling emotion
that stinks of disease, trucked its way into
my elbows and neck, which has tightened
as each minute of the show clicks by.

Ruined by the human condition,
exhausted with lust, these trumpets
spit blood at the hungry crowd,
baiting the savages to widen
their tongues.

For blood, for revenge, for sport.

NADIA ARIOLI

Where the Teeth Go

People have often told me that at the end of the world, we will all get our bodies back, and I believed them. But for some reason, I had always imagined it was our job to go find them. So if you died millions of years before the end, you'd have to search through deserts of dust to find the particles that once were yours. You'd have dig up old buildings to find your fingernails and scavenge through old sewers to get back your hair and fecal matter.

My own situation in this scenario would be less die, I imagined, because I had planned on being alive during the apocalypse or shortly before. It would be a simple matter of retracing my steps. Most of me would be in the three bathrooms I've inhabited over the years. I'd go through my old showers until I had a full set of hair and the toilets until my stomach was full. I'd go through my work and car to find the lopped-off fingernails and glue them back on. Bits of old skin from calluses and my lip would be lying around my apartment waiting to be reattached with grout.

For this reason primarily, I am uncomfortable with the idea of being an organ donor. Awkward conversations would ensue, and I would definitely lack the documentation to prove rightful ownership.

Except, I do lack my wisdom teeth due to my parents' advice and will die that way. I have no idea where they are kept now. At odd moments, I find myself hoping to god they're not ground into powder or abandoned in some dumpster like broken chairs.

I'd have to track down my oral surgeon and storm his office. I'd dig through his storage, and maybe there'd be an open safe where they're all kept, dusted and pristine. (Mine would be clearly labeled.) Then, I'd reach into my jaws and pop them back into place. But before I went up, maybe the surgeon would be there too except for a few of his ribs. Take back, he'd say, standing in front of his magnificent safe, *Take back all that you once knew...*

Some riddles solve themselves.

***

There's an old joke that makes me weep. Guy goes to the doctor and says "Hey doc, my brother's driving me crazy. He thinks he's a chicken!". And the doctor says "Well, why don't you turn him in?". And the guy goes "But doc, I need the eggs."

***

Woody Allen used that joke in a bit in Annie Hall about relationships, and that's probably true. I mean, I don't trust he has anything insightful to say about relationships. So anyways, that's what made the joke famous, I guess. But I don't think that's why it makes me weep. I think it has to do with the mad genius, more than love.

***

The mad genius is at best a bothersome trope. Oh he drinks and drinks but he is a genius, so we all put up with it. Like both are two sides of the coin. But even in a joke, he's still getting used. Would we really be friends with Van Gogh? Would we really get a beer with Beethoven? But we still insist they lay eggs for us.

***

The guy could have stuck his brother in a tower. The guy from the joke, I mean. Locked him up on an elaborate coop far above his house. Stacked up some pillows down below and collected the eggs each morning.

He's not really laying eggs though. That's the joke, of course. But we have to go along with it. A myth only works if you believe in it.

***

Doc goes into a joke, and it makes me old weep. Doctor says "Hey, chicken, my crazy is driving my brother. He thinks he's a guy." And the guy says "Well, why doesn't he turn you in?" and the doctor says "Well, you egg, I am needed."

***

We don't need teeth, when you think about it. Dentures are a thing and plenty of people have capps. The going rate is, 8 cents a molar, 10 cents a premolar, 5 a canine, and 12 an incisor. Put them under your pillow and wait.

***

We never had no tooth fairy.

***

I still don't know what came at night.

***

Doctor walks into a weep and makes a joke. Doctor says, "Hey, guy, my brother is driving me chicken. Guy thinks he's me." And the chicken says "Well, why don't I turn?" and the egg says "Well, we all want to eat her, late at night, please don't tell my wife."

Eggbeaters

Scientists have determined that riding a bicycle is impossible. To balance, one must be in motion. To be in motion, one must be balanced. And so, to teach children how to be extraordinary, parents give their tots tiny practice bikes for their hands. They place the hand bikes in sinks of water and go, go, go. Falling off is no matter; they get right back up. When the child is ready, they are presented with a proper bicycle. The parent or guardian whispers: This is a miracle, and no equation can explain it. But listen, once you perform the miracle, you'll never forget how.

HOWIE GOOD

Mean Dad Blues

Columbus, Ohio, wakes to rain. Overnight dad has drifted even further toward the big nothing. I try to make myself feel fittingly sad, but a heart, my heart, isn't like a bud that'll just open automatically, without inquiry or qualms. "Gangster of Love" is an old hit record by the Steve Miller Band. It's also now a job description. The work is more difficult than it sounds. When I walk, wherever I walk, my shadow walks ahead of me.

And Justice for All

The white police officer has too small a heart. How is that legal? the prosecutor asks. The wily old judge gestures that he can't hear over the roar of the rain. Witnesses in the case exchange anxious glances across the courtroom. The defense attorney just smirks. A while later, a van taking away the jurors runs completely off the road. No one is even hurt, but angels are everywhere, joking and shouting and smelling like turned earth.

Man, Woman, Birth, Death, Infinity

The ground is littered with used paper face masks. I want to shake this person and that person and tell them, "You can't be lost in your own world all the time." But, of course, I won't. A purplish darkness creeps over the city. I stream a movie about an international crew of astronauts on a journey to the cosmic womb. The ship malfunctions. Their sanity frays. They slowly turn against one another. Something out there in space is acting like a hulking bouncer who won't let them through. If they knew what I know, they would just chuckle. A month from now my daughter is having a daughter.

MATTHEW COOPER

What Causes Earth to Spin

For the truly colorfully sick amongst buskers and
Tree trimmers of all time, after flashbacks from all the
World's wars and all the great pillages—life's purpose is so
Simple that it is a Zen art: just to stay alive and watch
Our diaphragm rise and prove that the ghosts of
Crazy Horse and Custer are eternally drunk boxing
Over Montana in our hearts. See? Didn't you feel it just
                    Now?
Breathe—all the way in and don't exhale for a moment—
And that is where we all are. Somewhere between
Asphyxiation and freedom. Moment by moment and
Day by day as we ask if the world really does whirl at all or if
It's all of us walking on the ground that makes it spin from the
Pressure of the hundred billion of us infants mid-yawp jumping
Up and down in tears all these millennia wondering
If when we're gone the planet won't be able to sit still, have
Peace and quiet for a few billion years and watch the stars alone for once
Knowing all the kids staging cowboy and Indian battles have
Gone home for a while or at least somewhere else to annihilate
Themselves and laugh about it.
And there we will sit at our writing desks silently asking
Ourselves if tapping a pencil will make the words come out and
Transcribing the true meaning of life with the petrifying knowledge:
There may be none and the only certainty is the big circle
Around the moon on a cold night. You know the one. It tells
Us

Rain is coming.
But at some point
There will be no
One left for it to
Fall on. It seems
Peaceful.

Hourglass of Alexandria

For a time, you were a soldier
War having turned your hourglass
Upside down like the rest.
Except for you no bullets
Traced across the sky. You didn't
Lose any limbs. You never even fired
A shot, except at yourself over
And over and over again until you couldn't
Even march anymore. So, we think of
You as having died before you died.
We—your compatriots—lost track of you
When you were still here and on purpose
So that on your birthday we could just
Imagine you out there roaming in Mombasa—
Into the sunset with your war over—
Or perhaps somewhere else where you can be free
Brother.

Rainbow Bar Bathroom Mirror

I can't look in mirrors
Anymore and see a son
Only the remains
Of a father and how the one becomes
The other and so quick!—
How that knowledge makes
All the tears worth it and how
Death begs you to take the form
Of those who aren't here interminably
But whom must forever anyway
Be—
As I can stop chanting to god each day
Gonna make you pay for
That great big hole in my heart!
As my belly and My
Breast are whole again!
As everywhere I tread feels like
An Intercontinental Rainbow Bar basilica ballroom
Made just for me—the rambling ambassador
Son transmutable!

*Lines 13-14 are excerpts from "Your Time is Gonna Come",
Led Zeppelin I, Side Two, Track 1, Page—Jones—Plant

W.E. LEATHEM

Don't Hold Your Breath

And so on we go
holding our breath,
waiting on the next election
(to go *our* way),
awaiting the arrival

of our first child,
a parent's last,
oedipal breath

Watching the mail
with childlike eyes,
and unable to sleep,
anxious for Christmas,
for a postcard,
a catalogue,
for the tax return,
the sewer bill,
the census form…
that member invite from the ARP,
anything indicating
we haven't yet been forgotten

Dreading
another rainy season,
another go-round the Sun,
with its already set-in
deep-seated ennui

He was a great listener,
or so they'll say, a man
comfortable in his own skin

he could outlast a conversation,
holding out long after
the words caved in,
knowing that somewhere
there was more
still needing to be said

And never forget
that pride is a lean meal
and somber the realization,
that each act,
done and undone
will become a debt
to be repaid with interest

Winded

With a head like a pauper,
unfurl the crimson banner
to flail its foretelling
    of an ending

Vices abandoning ship,
ears ringing in the morning's breeze
the curse of regular employment
gawks one square in the eyes

So, go on
take out your change in fitful dreams
and though the kingdom of heaven awaits,
linger here awhile among
these pleasures of this world

exchanging hoped-for bliss
for the sure currency
of an instant's understanding

       more or less…

You Just Keep

(a little note to GHWB)

Hey man,
don't push me
I'm already moseying
as fast as I care to
as fast as I can

don't mind me
picking at the carcass
in the road,
pausing only long enough
to sniff at the rear end
of the moments slipping away

excuse me as i wipe
the echo of
the unpardonable sin
from my lips

swipe life's little plastic card
through the reader
of the cosmic check-out line

I've done my part:
piss'd on the neighbor's
prized orchids

And you just keep
bumping into me,

breathing stinky breath
down *my* neck,
tripping over *my* feet,
encroaching on *my* space
making *my* decisions uncomfortable
my comforts unlawful

And for what?
what is it about you
that makes you think
you can tell someone like me
(or any of a hundred million others)
what lines you ain't gonna let us cross?

You'd best back off

There's a frontier
I've not yet seen,
a road I really want to travel

And besides, what
have you to show
that hours bequeathed
you by fate
have not been
utterly, and completely wasted?

ED TATO

X-Rays

The kid in the flat
behind you wails through the wall while up
the street the panel beater's burglar alarm
howls with equal fervor
and equal likelihood of ending
no time soon.

The bells of St. Whoever
and your own internal echo
indicate the toddler is
a tick early tonight,
the red alert a tad late.

A tomcat scores the arm
of an armchair moldering on the porch,
pisses into the stuffing he's unstuffed,
bounds down, then up
at your window's Perspex
until assured its paw-sized aperture allows no ingress —
and so the skirling starts.

You flip your pillow
to find the new side just as lumpy.

The moon,
waxing or waning,
(and who can keep that straight?)
sheds more light than the bare globe strung from a wire
in this crypt the rental agent calls, *Your rooms.*
Neither moon nor globe illuminates
enough to read by,
but, as this is New Zealand,
one should take solace from the fact
that both are energy efficient —
though even absent flicker and hum
a low-watt fluorescent tube coiled to mimic a globe
displeases myriad ways,
as does the moldy-silled window —

however one might still,
contrary to your yowling cat companion,
rest assured after being told
no poisonous jumping spiders,
no venomous snakes loom here,
waiting to creep through
where flywire screens ought be —
and you squirm unconsoled, anyway, as nothing holds
back mosquitoes and blow flies whose droning
complacency unsettles so much more
than those phobias
or the noises you want to blame
for your own
unquiet insomnia.

Yellow Wind

That Christmas Eve I skipped
around wearing our Christmas stockings
my parents made me
sit on the couch and read
while the rest of them trimmed the tree.

The book was *Uncle Wiggily,*
about a rheumatic rabbit with a balloon
which sailed him around the world
and straight into the shit —

a balloon — like the fantastical skilligimink,
a made up color of a made up word —
that let me hope
I might escape Akron a while.

~

Mrs. Pierce was not the first
teacher to move me
from the trouble I caused,
consigning me and my desk
to each corner of the room
and then right beside her own desk,
but she succumbed
to failure best —
Bring a book, she said. *Read,*
take the tests, shut up, that's all.
Please.

I got through *Hot Corner Blues* and *Papillon*,
The Count of Monte Christo, all of Tolkien,
and 8th grade.

~

The first woman
I found to love me, read me
random poems in bed,
but troubles
followed just the same,

like they do
now, here
on a balcony
up against the outskirts of Quemado
where I scribble marginalia
through a Gideons Bible
until reddish particulates —
in a hue I know
as Ohio Cupboard Rust —
blow in from, let's say, the rodeo grounds,
or maybe from the calcified lake
and bluffs just beyond Omega —
they stain the canopy of Bianca's Last Stop Lodge,
vex my arms and legs,
and leave dull footprints inside
where I go to call the old man
and tell them I might make it
there, home, sometime
soon.

Zastrugi

After mittfulls of mushrooms
the golf course becomes tundra
crowned with frozen white waves
whose ice crusts crack as you clomp around,
as the dog sprints along,
sprints and skids
and stops and sniffs and starts.
You follow her blurred blue merle trails
as ice crystals flicker across all this whiteness.

You love that dog.

You've loved her
since you brought her home —
when she curled up by your feet,
then slept by your chair,
and wouldn't budge for food,
for water,
to do her business,
until the morning,
when you came down
to ask how she liked it here.
You come to a boulder
that has no business
in this or any other fairway.
You sit in the snow,
lean back,
watch her wander off,
as she does. As she did

in the wetlands
when she found the muskrat carcass,
as she did at Christopher Creek
when she first heard trumpeting elk.

Cold settles
on, in, all around you.

She's looked after you
as much as you have her,
like the time she lunged
at some drunk's crotch
and came away with a mouthful of shorts —
or the time in Portsmouth
when that self-proclaimed dog-whisperer
wouldn't fuck off, as you'd advised,
and she sprang and snapped
just scratching his jugular.
And each time, you said nothing,
just rubbed her chest once they'd gone.

You stretch through a yawn
as the wind picks up.

Portsmouth was after Utica, after Cayuga Lake,
after Buffalo, Columbus, Lawrence and Phoenix.

Before York,
before Acadia and back to York,
before Buffalo, Indy, Lawrence,
Arches, Canyonlands, the North Rim
and back to Lawrence.

Ten weeks in the truck,
both of you stinking like dead fish.

Just one last trip, you'd thought.

But instead off to Auckland
where she followed half a year later,
greeted by you and a month of quarantine,
then soon back here
again, once
Plans A through E flashed a cold shoulder.
She got back a week after you,
and, leaning against her crate,
ignored each Hiya, every Atta girl,
until, hackles raised, she turned
and glared, scowling,
as if to ask if you were done.

Stars fade
behind a fog of breath.

She crouches beside you, snarls then barks —
It's cold,
we want to go home.

ZARA LISBON

Carpe Noctum

I've been telling myself that a guy like you
doesn't deserve a poem by a girl like me
because wanting you means squandering all that I am
when to you
girls like me
are a dime a dozen.

But like a tick you're deep in the tissue of my brain
and you'll stay there forever if I don't make this cut
to let you out.

And I'd be lying if I said I never saw you coming.
Would you believe me if I said
a babysitter once read my palm and predicted you, the
wrench, opening up my life?
I was seven then and didn't like the thought of you
in a white t-shirt in the lobby of a doorman building on
the Upper East Side.
She told me you had money and came with a warning.
So, fifteen years later when
I was drinking apple martinis in a broken-mirrored room
on the corner of Hollywood Boulevard and saw you
standing in the accidental spotlight of a purposefully
crooked fixture
I was only half surprised.

It was the 9th of January and I had resolutions to roll
like a rolling stone.
They dared me to talk to you and I thought
carpe noctum.

Sorry

In a dream there was a polar bear man with a penguin on a
leash, and a girl I thought hated me put her arms around my
neck because she knew the penguin was dangerous. She had
tattoos of purple flowers on her wrists and I kept trying to say
sorry for all the things I had said behind her back.

Madison Avenue

I saw a mannequin lounging in a decked-out window
on Madison Avenue
rhinestones adhered to her white, white skin
and I was jealous of her because
of her wall-flat stomach and jutting hipbones
and because she didn't have to be real.

On the corner I overheard two homeless men
say that most of their dollar bills come from kids.
Kids are the generous ones, one said,
so I gave him fifteen dollars hoping maybe I could go back.

When I was a kid, I spent almost all my time
wondering what I'd be like as an adult.
I never thought in a million years
I'd spend almost all of my life remembering
what I was like as a child
and wanting to go back.

You sunk stakes into my brain
Set up camp in that gray terrain.
You talk of a theoretical girl
who is empty-headed in a charming way.
I'll hunt her down tear her limb from limb.

WAYNE F. BURKE

A Poem

sitting in a bar room nursing a bitter-tasting
beer when
Mahoney, whom I had not seen in
a coon's age, drops onto the stool
beside me:
pale blue eyes of regard, Anglo-face
bush of curly hair
and beard:
says he has been through every bookstore and
bar room in Cambridge looking for me: says
"what happened to your face?"
I tell him of my being beaten in a bar; tell
him I am going back there with a machine-gun.
He asks "so what else is new?"
I pull a sheet of paper from my pocket and
he reads the words typed on it.
"Best poem you ever wrote," he says.
I take another swallow of beer--
it tastes good.

Labor

first time in years
no labor for me
on Labor Day
I am free of the
factory and
looking forward to collecting
social security checks
unless they are
kept or
canceled by the
scamboogah in Washington
then I will go back
to work:
running a cash register at the
supermarket or
sweeping up over by the
cigarette machine, I do not know
what or
where
or care much
today, because
today I am working
on my tan.

First Book

since my first book was published
I feel as if I have grown
an inch or two,
added an additional foot to my
intestines;
more hair,
harder fingernails,
a darker shadow;
the future has more substance
to it, I want to hurry it
into existence;
but I fear
too
that it will all end
abruptly and
I will be on my back
in a hospital bed
in Marseilles or
elsewhere
and still
unilluminated.

NANCY KRIEG

lost and found

there is no us
save the feel of rhythm
blind hands wave in the dark
do not believe in wings
instead, there are legs
useless feet to march
shameless to the difference.

the mirrors move faster now
everyone enters, a facet
of the jewel we carve together.
that mirror moves too
it bursts a caped crusader
out of the phone booth.

every soul crawls like water
moving to the unsung cadence
crystalline sun warmed
they shape shift in harmony
over moss and rocks.
emerald trees cast shadows
in blue depths inside
a crystal ball.

to define the wind?
   the hush
of wings
where angels move
our wishes.

invention

feather
hops a sparrow
soars through azure space
floats   into my hand
scratches a sonnet.

feathers down the chief's back
many silent people   courage
honor   brave feather
still traveling through time.

the Egyptians weighed the heart
against feathers.
a balance of sharing   we remember
pieces of time   love has
played between our eyes.

feather   scribbles across the desert
sky   new fables and blues go down
awakening   to lightness
clarity   wisdom
the voice of one soul.

adventures of a wooden Indian

remember.
fingers of lightning
cracked the rain open,
that day, half asleep
my map blurred, the rainbow
eluded me. in that moment
I already existed. all of
us are agents, you can't stop love.
the ink dried on the pages
before I could save any more ideas.

believe.
the man selling words
smiled and sold out last week.
he is mute by choice
still sits in his booth
shakes hands with people
who give him money
they appreciate
his candor.

honor.
we could be a myth of children
come to gaze in honest eyes
an arc of pleasure
moving between hearts
where silence of the mind
and presence of reverence
bears a beauty
beyond human description.

R. NIKOLAS MACIOCI

At Flyers Pizza And Sub Shop

He wears a gold chain and the smugness
of youth. Ring and bracelet round out
his ensemble of jewelry. Because it is
a warm, early April day, he sports black
sleeveless t-shirt, well-worked biceps.

She perches across from him, turns profile.
I see her lovely face, its smooth contours.
Her hair hangs long, brown, and straight.
She has the beauty most women envy.

I try not to stare at them,
to detect flaws which I do when
they step outside to smoke.
With a turn of my head, I see them
out the front window. They could be
high school age or a little older.
I think I want them
porcelain perfect, or do I?
Truth is I resent their youth,
good looks, am a bit satisfied to see
porcelain crack. I assume they have sex.
That eliminates innocence.
Maybe I don't want them to have clean hearts.
Maybe I want glass to break, mercury to spill.

When I'm ready to leave, I try not to show effort
struggling from the booth.

H.C.

His bedroom is littered with broken dreams,
stacks of dirty laundry he stands ankle-deep in.

Down in the basement, he has rigged
a massage parlor, promises a healthy rub
down and a happy ending. Reared
in Southern Ohio poverty, he wants
to prove a success by placing hands
upon immodest needs of mostly married men.
A meager tax-free income of forty dollars
per client doesn't cancel destitution.

He smokes dollar-a-pack cigarettes,
lies about how his rich husband bought him
a car he can't afford to drive.

He does not squander middle age on hope,
buried during twenty years of caregiving
for five family members.

His modus operandi disincludes romantic
commitment. Aside from an occasional
hookup on the internet, he walks the earth
alone and makes love to what he can
easily let go of.

Hidden Guitar

I've hidden a guitar in the closet
between an old suitcase and two rifles
leaning against the back wall. I bought it
for $37.99 at Lev's Pawn Shop.
It's the color of a hard-blue January sky.

I don't know how to play one note.
I've never taken lessons. I just like
having it. Sometimes, I get teary-eyed
listening to guitar music, particularly
somber chords. A few times I've dragged
the guitar from the closet late at night,
strummed it like a waking weakness
to hug something to myself.

I love to sit in the dining room window
in the winter when it's snowing,
attempt to pick out a tune, vibration
of each string an amateurish incompetence
bumbling fingers fret.

Truth is, maybe I don't want to learn guitar.
Maybe joy comes from holding it close
to my chest where my dad once tied me
in a kitchen chair.

I don't want self-teaching books
or instruction from an expert.
I am the expert, the kid who once hid
in the closet because, at the time,
it seemed the safest place to be.

LINZI GARCIA

Open 7 a.m.

Sunrise drinking
stopped feeling
secretive and dirty
years ago.

I comfortably settle in
behind bar lights,
swallow my moral
ambiguity with the best
whiskey available at this dive,
which isn't great, but better
than the other tastes in my mouth.

I drink alone. A fucking shame.

That bar smell comforts me, this one less
stale with A/C running--
no such thing as spring
in Kansas.

Behind the bar,
books, records,
a bartender
untouched
for years.
We're all thirsty
for company.

Derailed

She knows she can count
on him for a good derailing--

taking the corner
too fast, tipping
too far into the wrong
direction, she crashes.

As she settles
into the chaos,
her disjointed
hips face the west,
chest points to the sky,
& gaze fixes on the east.

Twisted, she learns to love
the new perspective &
how the gravel digs
into her side.

He's found a comfortable spot
in the chaos,
stroking her wreck,
neither of them
claiming responsibility,
though they both
reap the benefit
of her inability
to move on.

Red's Cafe

Six years ago
I took my first pregnancy test
in this bathroom, after hours,
when I dated the ex-con
coffee-hop.

He's in Louisiana now,
but I'm still here,
the air freshener
still smells the same,
the hot water still
doesn't work, the lock's
still busted, and I still
have yet to get pregnant.

WILLIAM SHELDON

A Better Heaven

Sun and wind
wind on the water
leaves in the current
things a river tumbles
bleached white crawfish
shell of its former self
flake of flint worked
into a knife
cutting only current
coyote femur   heron feather
and someday perhaps me
or you if time
catches you
Upstream you tumble
breathless on some gravel bar
begin your slow exchange
with the world
Maybe those who'd
look for you are gone
so no one finds you
High water dislodges
some part of you
tibia say or ulna
to return the way you came
A canoeist more interested
in seducing a rowing mate
than lessons lifts you
holds you up
drops you in the shallows
to wait
for the next high water

Funereal

We donned our death hair,
read the rain maps,
and hied on a hawk's wind
down to Deep river,
with its mud musk and dust
broth, its sad smothered
sun under clouds, parting
for a fingernail moon
to scratch the hair-ash
streets, and starlit water
snakes whipsawing the current
where the mud-toothed river
chewed the town's brink.

Death herons rose
cacophonous, chorale-throated
in the creosote wind
whining through salt cedar
while grass marched
on pampas legs
toward destiny undreamt,
the end of the engine-
throated river.

Preordained under moon-throb
we dragged the drossy body
to the mossy font
dressed in daily togs,
fingernails dirty and unpared:

spare words in the silt rot,
dipped and dropped
in a reedy canoe, taken
into the river-grip,
the grass-walk, downstream.
"These are the days,"
we say, burning our hair
in Deep River's streets.

I'd Like to Be There

at the last of people
some evening when the sky
looks like now
through this airport window
trees still green reaching
into rich clouds unaware
of our passing
to sit behind this glass
in a concourse bereft
of passengers
watching late afternoon sun
waiting for some flock
to find this square of blue
I want to rise and walk out
the front door that still
slides open into the day's
heavy humidity
into coming night finding
my way to the interstate
in unrequited love
with the quiet
last man on the road
both crumbling
and happy to

The Players:

M.J. (Michael Joseph) Arcangelini was born 1952 in western Pennsylvania. He has resided in northern California since 1979. His work has been published in many magazines, online journals, over a dozen anthologies, & 5 collections, the newest of which is "A Quiet Ghost" from Luchador Press, 2020.

Nadia Arioli (nee Wolnisty) is the co-founder and editor in chief of *Thimble Literary Magazine*. Their work has appeared or is forthcoming in *Spry, SWWIM, Apogee, Penn Review, McNeese Review, Kissing Dynamite, Bateau, Heavy Feather Review, Whale Road Review, Poetry South,* and others. They have chapbooks from Cringe-Worthy Poetry Collective, Dancing Girl Press, Spartan, and a full-length from Luchador.

Rob Azevedo is a writer and radio host from Manchester NH. His first book of poetry was released in January 2021 called *Turning On The Wasp.*

Tohm Bakelas is a social worker in a psychiatric hospital. He was born in New Jersey, resides there, and will die there. His poems have appeared in numerous journals, zines, and online publications. He is the author of several chapbooks, one full length book of poetry, and his work has been nominated several times for the Pushcart Prize. He is also the editor of Between Shadows Press.

Jason Baldinger is from Pittsburgh and misses roaming the country writing poems. His newest book is *A Threadbare Universe* (Kung Fu Treachery Press), as well as the forthcoming *The Afterlife is a Hangover* (Stubborn Mule Press) and *A History of Backroads Misplaced* (Kung Fu Treachery). His work has been published widely across print journals and online. You can hear him read his work on Bandcamp and on lp's by The Gotobeds and Theremonster.

Rusty Barnes lives in Revere MA with his wife and children. A lifelong poet and crime writer, he is the author of fifteen books of fiction and poetry including the forthcoming chapbook *Dear So and So*, from Analog Submission Press. He co-edits *Live Nude Poems* with his wife, the poet Heather Sullivan, and oversees *TOUGH*, a blogazine of crime fiction and occasional reviews.

James Benger is the author of two fiction ebooks, and three chapbooks, two full-lengths, and coauthor of four split books of poetry. He is on the Board of Directors of The Writers Place and the Riverfront Readings Committee, and is the founder of the *365 Poems In 365 Days* online workshop, and is Editor In Chief of the subsequent anthology series. He lives in Kansas City with his wife and children.

Luis Cuauhtemoc Berriozabal is the author of *Make the Water Laugh* from Rogue Wolf Press. He works in the mental health field in Los Ángeles. His poetry has appeared in *Blue Collar Review, Kendra Steiner Editions, Mad Swirl, Unlikely Stories,* and *Yellow Mama Webzine*.

Mela Blust is a trauma survivor, and a mother. Since seeking publication just over a year ago, Mela's work has been nominated twice for Best of the Net, and has appeared or is forthcoming in *The Bitter Oleander, Rust+Moth, The Nassau Review, The Sierra Nevada Review, South Florida Poetry Journal, Collective Unrest,* and many more. Her debut poetry collection, *Skeleton Parade,* is available with Apep Publications and her second collection, *They Found a Woman's Body,* is available with Vegetarian Alcoholic Press. She is a contributing editor for *Barren Magazine,* and can be followed at https://twitter.com/melablust

Ace Boggess is author of six books of poetry, including *Escape Envy* (forthcoming from Brick Road Poetry Press), *The Prisoners*, and *I Have Lost the Art of Dreaming It So*. His poems have appeared in *Michigan Quarterly Review, Harvard Review, J Journal, North Dakota Quarterly*, and other journals. An ex-con, he lives in Charleston, West Virginia, where he writes and tries to stay out of trouble.

Charlie Brice won the 2020 *Field Guide Magazine* Poetry Contest. His chapbook, *All the Songs Sung* (Angel Flight Press), and his fourth poetry collection, *The Broad Grin of Eternity* (WordTech) arrived in 2021. His poetry has been nominated for the Best of Net Anthology and three times for a Pushcart Prize and has appeared in *The Atlanta Review, Chiron Review, The Paterson Literary Review, The Sunlight Press, Sparks of Calliope*, and elsewhere.

Steve Brisendine is a writer, poet, occasional artist and recovering journalist from Mission, Kansas. His poetry has appeared in the most recent volume of the *365 Days* Poets anthology, as well as *Squawk Back, Grand Little Things* and *The Rye Whiskey Review*. His first poetry collection, *The Words We Do Not Have*, was published in spring 2021 from Spartan Press.

Michael H. Brownstein's latest volumes of poetry, *A Slipknot to Somewhere Else* (2018) and *How Do We Create Love?* (2019), were published by Cholla Needles Press.

Wayne F. Burke's poetry has appeared in a wide variety of publications online and in print. He is author of seven published full-length poetry collections. The most recent, *ESCAPE FROM THE PLANET CROUTON*, published by Luchador Press, 2019. His poem "Prepositioned" was nominated for "Best of the Net." His poem "Max" won Poem of the Year Honorable Mention from *The Song Is... magazine*.

A collection of his short stories, titled "TURMOIL & Other Stories," was published by Adelaide Press, NY, 2020. He is currently at work on a hybrid of memoir/novel. He has lived for the past thirty-five years in the central Vermont region, USA.

John Clayton is the current Poet Laureate of Belle, Missouri.

Paul Cordeiro, a retired shoe salesman, has been mistaken for John Malkovich, once, while driving a shuttle from a used tire warehouse to an outdoor mall. Before facial recognition apparatus, woman, shoehorned into pumps, allegedly fantasized that he was a miniature Al Bundy. People appear larger within screens. His verse also appears this year at *1870, Gray Sparrow Journal, Heroin Love Songs, Seppuku Quarterly, Sophisticated Chaos.* In 2021 Analog Submission Press, released a second limited-run chapbook, *Do Not Touch.*

Matt Cooper is an English and creative writing major at Wichita State University. He has written and contributed to the *Butler Lantern, Butler County Times-Gazette,* and the *WSU Sunflower* newspapers as well as written poems that appeared in the *Mikrokosmos* literary journal. While pursuing a masters degree in poetry, Cooper has studied the Japanese language and literature at great length. He hopes to one day take residence in Katano, Osaka, Japan.

John Dorsey lived for several years in Toledo, Ohio. He is the author of several collections of poetry, including *Teaching the Dead to Sing: The Outlaw's Prayer* (Rose of Sharon Press, 2006), *Sodomy is a City in New Jersey* (American Mettle Books, 2010), *Tombstone Factory* (Epic Rites Press, 2013), *Appalachian Frankenstein* (GTK Press, 2015) *Being the Fire* (Tangerine Press, 2016) and *Shoot the Messenger* (Red Flag Poetry, 2017), *Your Daughter's Country* (Blue

Horse Press, 2019), and *Which Way to the River: Selected Poems 2016-2020* (OAC Books, 2020). His work has been nominated for the Pushcart Prize, Best of the Net, and the Stanley Hanks Memorial Poetry Prize. He was the winner of the 2019 Terri Award given out at the Poetry Rendezvous. He may be reached at archerevans@ yahoo.com.

Holly Day has been a writing instructor at the Loft Literary Center in Minneapolis since 2000. Her poetry has recently appeared in Asimov's *Science Fiction, Grain*, and *Harvard Review* and her newest full-length collections are *Into the Cracks* (Golden Antelope Press), *Cross Referencing a Book of Summer* (Silver Bow Publishing), *The Tooth is the Largest Organ in the Human Body* (Anaphora Literary Press), and *Book of Beasts* (Weasel Press). To find out more visit www.hollylday.blogspot.com.

James H Duncan is the editor of *Hobo Camp Review* and the author of *We Are All Terminal But This Exit Is Mine, Feral Kingdom*, and *Beyond the Wounded Horizon*, among other books of poetry and fiction. He currently resides in upstate New York and reviews indie bookshops at his blog, *The Bookshop Hunter*. For more, visit www.jameshduncan.com.

Alexis Rhone Fancher has been published in *Best American Poetry, Rattle, Hobart, Verse Daily, Plume, Tinderbox, Cleaver, Diode, The American Journal of Poetry, Nashville Review, Poetry East,* and elsewhere. She's authored six poetry collections, most recently, *Junkie Wife* (Moon Tide Press, 2018), and *The Dead Kid Poems* (KYSO Flash Press, 2019). *EROTIC: New & Selected* (NYQ Books) dropped in March, 2021, and her seventh collection, *Entra qui*, will publish (in Italian) from Edizioni Ensemble, Italia in mid-2021. Her photographs are featured worldwide including the covers of *Witness,* and *The Pedestal Magazine*. A multiple Pushcart Prize and Best of the Net nominee, Alexis is poetry editor of *Cultural Daily*. www.alexisrhonefancher.com

Linzi Garcia is the author of *Thank You* & *Live A Great Story*. She is the publicist for Meadowlark Press & Anamcara Press, & she teaches at Emporia State University.

Victoria Garton has been writing and publishing poetry for a number of years. A recent Riverfront Poetry Series, Rattle Current Events, and Phil Miller Scholarship reader, her work has been in *River City Poetry*, *Phoebe*, *Quarterly West*, *Poem*, and *The Sow's Ear Poetry Review*. Recent acceptances include *Thorny Locust* and *I-70 Review*. Her book *Kisses in the Raw Night* was published by BkMk Press, U.M.K.C.

Tony Gloeggler a life-long resident of New York City and managed group homes for the mentally challenged as my life's work. My work has appeared in *Rattle, Nerve Cowboy, BODY, New Ohio Review, Trailer Par Quarterly* & *Black Coffee Review*. My full length books include *One Wish Left* (Pavement Saw Press 2002) and *Until The Last Light Leaves* (NYQ Books 2015). NYQ Books published *What Kind Of Man* in June 2020

Howie Good, Ph.D., a professor of journalism at SUNY New Paltz, is the author of more than a dozen poetry collections, including most recently *The Death Row Shuffle* (Finishing Line Press), *The Trouble with Being Born* (Ethel Micro Press), and *Gunmetal Sky* (Thirty West Publishing).

Tim Heerdink is the author of *Somniloquy & Trauma in the Knottseau Well, The Human Remains, Red Flag and Other Poems, Razed Monuments, Checking Tickets on Oumaumua, Sailing the Edge of Time, I Hear a Siren's Call, Ghost Map, A Cacophony of Birds in the House of Dread,* and short stories, *The Tithing of Man* and *HEA-VEN2*. His poems appear in various journals and anthologies. He is the President of Midwest Writers Guild of Evansville, Indiana.

Paul Koniecki reads everyday and wants to meet the world with curiosity and poems.

Nancy Krieg lives in Kansas City, MO where creating is cherished. She works as a job coach for developmentally disabled adults. She has been seen in jazz and blues clubs and sometimes art museums behind a drum kit, a djembe, or a mandolin. Now, she has turned her eye toward poetry because punching keys or even mandolin strings is so much easier than moving drums around.

w.e. leathem - co-founder and co-owner of KC's notorious indie bookstore Prospero's Books and co-founder and executive publisher of Spartan Press, Leathem is a penner of yarns, verse and nonfictions. His 4th collection of poetry *Old Goat* will appear on Spartan Press before mid-year. He lives in the hinterlands of KC with his partner, his son and step daughters and a hearty assortment of beasts ...

Brenda Linkeman has been coordinating the renovation of the Rolla Public Library pocket park, which will include a stage. She has visions of poetry readings, plays, and concerts when the renovation is complete. She is a child therapist and has also taught art to children, both in Texas, and in Missouri from her home art studio, "Expressions!." Poetry and art have been a consistent part of her life.

Zara Lisbon is the author of *Fake Plastic Girl* and *Fake Plastic World. Baby's First Apocalypse* is her first book of poetry.

R. Nikolas Macioci earned a PhD from The Ohio State University, and for thirty years taught for the Columbus City Schools. In addition to English, he taught Drama and developed a Writers Seminar for select students. OCTELA, the Ohio

Council of Teachers of English, named Nik Macioci the best secondary English teacher in the state of Ohio. Nik is the author of eleven books. *Cafes of Childhood* (the original chatbook with additional poems), critics and judges called a "beautifully harrowing account of child abuse," but not "sentimental" or "self-pitying," an "amazing book," and "a single unified whole." *Cafes of Childhood* was submitted for the Pulitzer Prize in 1992. In 2021, he was nominated for a Pushcart Prize. In addition, more than two hundred of his poems have been published here and abroad in magazines and journals, including *The Society of Classical Poets Journal, Chiron, Concho River Review, The Bombay Review, Tipton Poetry Journal,* and *Blue Unicorn.*

John Macker grew up in Colorado and has lived in New Mexico for 25 years. He has published 13 full-length books and chapbooks of poetry, 2 audio recordings, an anthology of fiction and essays, and several broadsides over 30 years. His most recent are *Atlas of Wolves, The Blues Drink Your Dreams Away, Selected Poems 1983-2018,* (a 2019 Arizona/New Mexico Book Awards finalist), *Desert Threnody,* essays and short fiction, *El Rialto,* a short prose memoir and *Chaco Sojourn,* a short story, (both illustrated by Leon Loughridge and published by Dry Creek Art Press.) In 2019, his poem "Happiness" won a Fischer Poetry Prize finalist citation, sponsored by the Telluride Institute. His manuscript of new poems, *the disinterred light is* in progress. He lives with his artist wife Annie and two mutts, Ruby Tuesday and Sean O'Casey.

Arturo Mantecón is a poet and literary translator whose poems have appeared in various reviews and anthologies. His books of translation include three volumes of the collected works of Leopoldo María Panero and selected works by Francisco Ferrer Lerín and Mario Santiago Papasquiaro. *Before the Night Comes,* a collection of poems by one of his heteronyms, José Primitivo Charlevoix, will be published this year by Nomadic Press.

Jason Mayer spent the first part of his adult life as a Marine Corps Combat Correspondent covering stories on five continents and more than 50 countries. After leaving the Marine Corps, he spent eight years working with a government publishing contractor managing the development of more than 200 annual publishing projects. Today, he is co-owner of Milcon Systems, Inc., a company that designs, builds, and sells playgrounds and recreational construction projects. Some of Jason's other printed works include: *Parables of Lucas Fosterman, Barber | Chef | Ripper, Parables of Sarah Blackstone, Fuzzy Dragons* and *Wild Yetis,* and *Reported for Duty.*

Marc Olmsted has appeared in *City Lights Journal, New Directions in Prose & Poetry, New York Quarterly, The Outlaw Bible of American Poetry* and a variety of small presses. He is the author of five collections of poetry, including *What Use Am I a Hungry Ghost?,* which has an introduction by Allen Ginsberg. Olmsted's 25 year relationship with Ginsberg is chronicled in his Beatdom Books memoir *Don't Hesitate: Knowing Allen Ginsberg 1972-1997 - Letters and Recollections,* available on Amazon. For more of his work, http://www.marcolmsted.com

Shawn Pavey is the author of *Talking to Shadows* (Main Street Rag Press, 2008), *Nobody Steals the Towels From a Motel 6* (Spartan Press, 2015), and *Survival Tips for the Pending Apocalypse* (2019, Spartan Press) which was 1st runner up for the 2020 Thorpe Menn Literary Excellence Award. He co-founded *The Main Street Rag Literary Journal* and served as an Associate Editor. His infrequently updated blog is at www.shawnpavey.com. His books can be purchased from him signed and/or personalized at https://shawn-pavey-poet.square.site/ or wherever one prefers to buy books online.

Linnet Phoenix is a poet born in Scotland, raised in Sussex and currently resides in a village in North Somerset, UK. Her work has been published in several places including *Impspired Magazine, New*

Verse News, Punk Noir Magazine, Heroin Love Songs, Rusty Truck
and *Open Skies Quarterly*. Her chapbook *Rusty Stars* was published
by Between Shadows Press. Her first full collection *Urban Mustang*
will be published by Impspired in the summer of 2021. Her second
chapbook will also be released later in 2021 from Newington Blue
Press. When not writing she also enjoys horse-riding in rainstorms.

Tanya Rakh was born on the outskirts of time and space in a
cardboard box. After extensive planet-hopping, she currently makes
her home near Houston, Texas where she writes poetry, surrealist
prose, and cross-genre amalgamations. Her writing has appeared in
numerous journals including *Redshift 4, Literary Orphans, Heroin
Love Songs, Fearless, Yes, Poetry*, and *The Rye Whiskey Review*. Tanya
is the author of two books: *Hydrogen Sofi* (Hammer & Anvil Books
2019) and *Wildflower Hell* (Rogue Wolf Press 2021).

Linda Rocheleau is a veteran teacher, writer and poet living
in Asheville, North Carolina. Recent publications include: *Trailer
Park Quarterly, Savannah Literary Journal* and others.

William Sheldon lives with his family in Hutchinson, Kansas
where he teaches and writes. He took his BS andMA in English
from Emporia State University and an MFA inCreative Writing
from Wichita State University. His poetry has been published
widely in such journals as *Blue Mesa Review, Columbia, Epoch
Prairie Schooner,* and *Quiddity.* He is the author of two books of
poetry, *Retrieving Old Bones* (Woodley) and *Rain Comes Riding*
(Mammoth) as well as a chapbook, *Into Distant Grass* (Oil
Hill). *Retrieving Old Bones* was a Kansas City Star Noteworthy
Book and is listed as one of the Great Plains Alliance's Great
Books of the Great Plains. He plays bass for the band The
Excuses.

Scott Silsbe was born in Detroit. He now lives in Wilkinsburg, Pennsylvania. His poems and prose have appeared in numerous periodicals and have been collected in the three books: *Unattended Fire, The River Underneath the City,* and *Muskrat Friday Dinner.* He is also an assistant editor at Low Ghost Press.

Ed Tato lives in Seaford, Australia with his wife and daughter. His poems abide in various books, print journals and websites. They wait—painted under the floorboards of a bedroom in Lawrence, Kansas—crumpled by the toilet on the bus from Eureka to El Dorado—for someone, anyone, to find, to read, to pause and say, yes, that's about right, I kind of thought that, too.

William Taylor Jr. lives and writes in San Francisco, California. He is the author of numerous books of poetry, and a volume of fiction. His work has been published widely in journals across the globe, including *Rattle, The New York Quarterly,* and *The Chiron Review.* He is a five-time Pushcart Prize nominee and was a recipient of the 2013 Kathy Acker Award. *Pretty Things to Say,* (Six Ft. Swells Press, 2020) is his latest collection of poetry.

Brett Lars Underwood is the author of two books: *MUSH* and *MUSHARONA.*

Julie Valin has been writing poetry since Ditto jeans and arcades were a thing. Her poems have appeared in *The Black Shamrock, The Poeming Pigeon, Chiron Review, Red Fez,* and more, plus several anthologies & collections, including the Punk Rock Chapbook series by Epic Rites Press. She is also a book designer for her business, Self to Shelf Publishing Services, and a co-founder of the celebrated after-hours poetry press, Six Ft. Swells. She has a penchant for books, the moon, art, birdsong, the Blues, indie-everything, a good burrito and a cold beer. She lives in Northern California with her husband and daughter.

George Wallace is writer in residence at the Walt Whitman Birthplace, author of 38 chapbooks of poetry, and a prominent member of the NYC poetry performance scene. Honored internationally for his work, he travels nationwide to share his poetry and has had recent visits to writing communities in Kansas City, St Louis, Oklahoma City, San Antonio, Albuquerque and Taos, NM.

Merritt Waldon is the Co-Author of *Oracles From A Strange Fire*, with Ron Whitehead, recently published by Cajun Mutt Press.

Francine Witte's poetry and fiction have appeared in *Smokelong Quarterly, Wigleaf, Mid-American Review*, and *Passages North*. Her latest books are *Dressed All Wrong for This* (Blue Light Press), *The Way of the Wind* (AdHoc fiction), and *The Theory of Flesh* (Kelsay Books.) Her chapbook, *The Cake, The Smoke, The Moon* (flash fiction) will be published by ELJ September, 2021. She is flash fiction editor for Flash Boulevard and The South Florida Poetry Journal. She lives in NYC.

This project was made possible, in part, by generous
support from the Osage Arts Community.

Osage Arts Community provides temporary time, space
and support for the creation of new artistic works in a
retreat format, serving creative people of all kinds —
visual artists, composers, poets, fiction and nonfiction
writers. Located on a 152-acre farm in an isolated rural
mountainside setting in Central Missouri and bordered
by ¾ of a mile of the Gasconade River, OAC provides
residencies to those working alone, as well as welcoming
collaborative teams, offering living space and workspace
in a country environment to emerging and mid-career
artists. For more information, visit us at www.osageac.org

Osage Arts Community

CPSIA information can be obtained
at www.ICGtesting.com
Printed in the USA
BVHW031612230821
615012BV00007B/257

9 781952 411700